Social Reconstruction Through Education

The Philosophy, History, and Curricula of a Radical Ideal

SOCIAL AND POLICY ISSUES IN EDUCATION: THE DAVID C. ANCHIN SERIES

KATHRYN M. BORMAN, *SERIES EDITOR*

Basil Bernstein: Consensus and Controversy
edited by Alan R. Sadovnik

Critical Education for Work: Multidisciplinary Approaches
edited by Richard D. Lakes

Children Who Challenge the System
edited by Anne M. Bauer and Ellen M. Lynch

Contemporary Issues in U.S. Education
edited by Dolores Stegelin

Critical Education for Work: Multidisciplinary Approaches
edited by Richard D. Lakes

Effective Schooling for Disadvantaged Students: School-based Strategies for Diverse Student Populations
edited by Howard Johnston and Kathryn M. Borman

Home Schooling: Political, Historical, and Pedagogical Perspectives
edited by Jan Van Galen and Mary Anne Pitman

Investing in U.S. Schools: Directions for Educational Policy
edited by Bruce A. Jones and Kathryn M. Borman

Minority Education: Anthropological Perspectives
edited by Evelyn Jacob and Cathie Jordan

Social Reconstruction Through Education: The Philosophy, History, and Currcula of a Radical Ideal
edited by Michael E. James

IN PREPARATION

Assessment, Testing, and Evaluation in Teacher Education
edited by Suzanne W. Soled

SOCIAL RECONSTRUCTION THROUGH EDUCATION

THE PHILOSOPHY, HISTORY, AND CURRICULA OF A RADICAL IDEAL

edited by

Michael E. James

Ablex Publishing Corporation
Norwood, New Jersey

Copyright © 1995 by Ablex Publishing Corporation

All rights reserved. No part of this publication may be reproduced, stored in a retrieval system, or transmitted, in any form or by any means, electronic, mechanical, photocopying, microfilming, recording, or otherwise, without permission of the publisher.

Printed in the United States of America

Library of Congress Cataloging-in-Publication Data

Social reconstruction through education : the philosophy, history, and curricula of a radical ideal / edited by Michael E. James.
      p. cm.—(Social and policy issues in education)
  Includes bibliographical references and indexes.
  ISBN 0-89391-924-1.—ISBN 1-56750-145-1 (ppk.)
  1. Educational sociology—United States—History—20th century.
  2. Progressive education—United States—History—20th century.
  3. Education—United States—Philosophy—History—20th century.
  I. James, Michael E. II. Series.
LC191.4S656 1994
370.19—dc20   94-38595
                                                                   CIP

Ablex Publishing Corporation
355 Chestnut Street
Norwood, New Jersey 07648

A Dream

The light—so dim it drew the horizon near—
Showed giant figures, almost human, hemming me round,
Faceless or with averted faces. I stood alone and I could hear
Their almost human voices—impressive sound
Well-amplified, most high fidelity—commanding "Kneel!"
I did not kneel. And from me came a bleat—
Most poorly modulated, low fidelity—"I do not feel
Your right to make me kneel." Came their repeat
"Kneel!"—computer-programmed, nuclear-driven now—"We
  have the power.
We are the nations, churches, collectivities.
You are a piece of us—without us, nothing. In this dark hour
Of dire emergency, to stand upright is treason, sacrilege—
  down on your knees!"
Darkness had further dimmed the scene and it was cold.
Wavering, my voice came to   my ears, perhaps into their almost
  human ears, whispering "No!"
From near around me, like a significant secret told
By friend to friend in private, came fellow-sounds—at first low
Then amplified by human power—a chorus free
Praising man and singing, "No!" Above me dawned a dim but
  brightening star.
I saw faces of men—a company of little men standing tall and
  welcoming me.
Now there was light enough to fling the horizon far.

—Kenneth D. Benne

TABLE OF CONTENTS

List Of Contributors   **ix**

Introduction   **xiii**

Prologue   **xxi**

1   Is Social Transformation Always Progressive? Rightist Reconstructions Of Schooling Today
Michael W. Apple   **1**

2   The Social Frontier 1934–1943: Retrospect And Prospect
James M. Giarelli   **27**

3   "Red Teachers Can't Save Us": Radical Educators And Liberal Journalists In The 1930s
James Wallace   **43**

4   Harold Rugg's Social Reconstructionism
Peter F. Carbone and
Virginia S. Wilson   **57**

5   Female Founders And The Progressive Paradox
Susan F. Semel   **89**

6   Southern Progressivism During The Great Depression: Virginia And African-American Social Reconstruction
Michael James   **109**

7   Social Reconstructionism For 21st-Century Educators
William O. Stanley and
Kenneth D. Benne   **139**

Author Index   **173**

Subject Index   **177**

LIST OF CONTRIBUTORS

Michael W. Apple is John Bascom Professor of Curriculum and Instruction and Educational Policy Studies at the University of Wisconsin, Madison. Among his most recents books are *Official Knowledge: Democratic Education in a Conservative Age* (1993) and *Democratic Schools* (1995).

Peter F. Carbone, Jr. is Professor of the Practice of Education at Duke University, where he has served at various times as an Assistant Dean in the undergraduate college of arts and sciences, Director of Student Teaching, Director of the MAT Program, Director of Graduate Studies in Education, and Chair of the Education Department. His writings include *The Social and Educational Thought of Harold Rugg*, *Value Theory and Education*, and numerous articles. He is past president of the South Atlantic Philosophy of Education Society.

Kenneth D. Benne was Professor Emeritus, Boston University. For 20 years prior to his retirement he was Berenson Professor of Human Relations. He was the author of numerous books including *A Conception of Authority*, *Education for Tragedy*, and *The Task of Post-Contemporary Education*. He died in October, 1992 at the age of 84.

James M. Giarelli is Associate Professor of Philosophy and Education and Chair, Department of Educational Theory, Policy, and Administration in the Graduate School of Education, Rutgers University. He is editor of *Philosophy of Education 1988* and co-editor with Peter McLaren of *Critical Theory and Educational Research*. He has published widely in social philosophy, ethics and educational philosophy and serves as associate editor of *Educational Theory*.

Michael E. James is Associate Professor of Education and Chair, Department of Education, Connecticut College. He is presently serving as Assistant Dean of National and International Programs. He is author of numerous articles on the history of curriculum and progressive education. He is currently completing a comparative study of the history of schooling and the civil rights movement in the far West and South.

Susan F. Semel is an Assistant Professor of Education at Hofstra University. She received her A.B. in European history from Wheaton College, and her M.A.T., in Ed.M. and Ed.D. in history and philosophy of education from Teachers College, Columbia University. Dr. Semel taught history at the Dalton School from 1965 to 1988. Her current research interests include the history of progressive education, international educational reform, and the history of women and education. She is co-editor of the *International Handbook of Educational Reform*, the author of *The Dalton School: The Transformation of a Progressive School*, and the co-author of the forthcoming *Exploring Education*

William O. Stanley III received his Ph.D. in the philosophy of education from the University of Illinois in 1974. His dissertation analyzed the U.S. communist party and its approach to education during the 1930s. In addition to his other publications, he co-authored a paper with his father, William O. Stanley, in 1977 on John Dewey and the social subjects.

James Wallace is Professor of Eduction at Lewis and Clark College in Portland, OR. His degrees are from Earlham College, Haverford College, and Harvard University. He directed the Reed College Master of Arts in Teaching Program for 6 years. He is author of *Liberal Journalism and American Education, 1914–1941*, and co-author of *Social and Ethical Issues in Professional Education*.

Virginia S. Wilson is Head of the Department of Humanities at the North Carolina School of Science and Mathematics and an Adjunct Assistant Professor in the Education and Master of Arts in Teaching Programs at Duke University. She is co-editor of *Teaching Social Studies: Handbook of Trends, Issues, and Implications for the Future.*

ACKNOWLEDGMENTS

This collection of essays would not have been possible without the encouragement of Kenneth Benne and James Wallace. Ken believed social reconstruction deserved continual revisiting. Jim must be thought of as my co-editor, although he will undoubtedly refuse such a title. His questions, comments, and editorial assistance were invaluable.

INTRODUCTION

Michael James
Connecticut College

In 1989, I asked Kenneth Benne, James Wallace, and James Giarelli to join me in a seminar on "Social Reconstruction" for the annual fall meeting of the American Educational Studies Association in Toronto, Canada. Benne, professor emeritus from Boston University, was one of the few remaining "reconstructionists" from the depression decade of the 1930s. The discussion that grew from the panel that morning was animated, invigorating, and affirming, and Benne was at the center of the dialogue. The audience sought his opinion and he responded with candor and the knowledge one would expect from someone who had lived the movement for decades.

Often, professional meetings have their greatest benefit after the formal panels and papers have concluded. Such was the case in Toronto. Sitting at Ken's side during the dinner and informal talk that followed the panel remains one of the real pleasures of my professional life. Ken told us stories that ranged from his meetings with John Dewey and William Kilpatrick to his cogent and biting commentary on the conservative ascendancy during the Reagan years. Later, he encouraged me to put the essays from the Toronto meeting together as a book. Along with additional contributions by other scholars, this volume on the history and philosophy of social reconstruction is the result of Ken's encouragement. The essays are dedicated to his memory, for he died on October 8, 1992 at the age of 84.

Benne's professional years, spanning some six decades, were innovative, productive, and above all else, inspirational. Before his death, Paul Nash prepared a biography on Ken. Benne was one of the founders of the Philosophy of Education Society and a cofounder of the NTL Institute of Applied Behavioral Science. During his lengthy career, he was a coinventor of the T-group, or training group. He held the Kilpatrick Award for his contributions to American philosophy as well as the Distinguished Alumnus Award from Teachers College.[1]

His early life was spent on a farm in Kansas where he learned from his parents the values that guided his life and work. He taught high school after attending Kansas State, then took graduate degrees from the University of Michigan and Teachers College, Columbia University, in philosophy and the philosophy of education. For 20 years he was Berenson Professor of Human Relations at Boston University, where he founded and directed the Human Relations Center.

His scholarly writings are too numerous to mention here; Paul Nash described them as "covering twenty pages of single-spaced print." The three that I most easily associate with the corpus of Ken's work are *A Conception of Authority* (1943), *Education for Tragedy* (1967) and *The Task of Post-Contemporary Education* (1990). It was Ken's writing, along with Theodore Brameld and the contemporary reconstructionists such as Michael Apple and Paulo Friere, that have most clearly articulated for me (as I am sure for others) how schooling can and should enable democracy.

Ken's contribution to this volume comes in two parts. First, he and William O. Stanley III, the son of Kenneth's long-time friend and colleague, William O. Stanley, collaborated on Chapter 7, "Social Reconstructionism for 21st-Century Educators." Sadly, some 3 months after Ken's passing, the senior William O. Stanley died at the age of 90. Stanley taught for years at the University of Illinois, where he served as Chair of the Department of History and Philosophy of Education. His writings, like Ken's, are too numerous to mention here but include the well-known *Education and Integration* (1952) and *Fundamentals of Curriculum Development* (with B.O. Smith & J.H. Shores, 1950). The Benne and Stanley chapter is a fitting conclusion to the book, for it dis-

---

[1] The Benne biography was reprinted in the *NTL Institute* news release announcing his death in October 1992.

cusses the philosophical and historical connections of reconstruction, especially the contribution made by Karl Mannheim and Max Weber. Benne and Stanley situate technology, planning, and mass action within reconstructionist thought and practice. The notion that reconstruction is a naïve and therefore untenable solution to the crisis of the modern and now postmodern world is clearly refuted by Benne and Stanley. Their notion is of a democratic society through education and re-education, as their definition of democracy goes far beyond annualized elections and petty party politics to include unfettered, collective participation, planning—an old notion that still rings true—and the communal uses of technology. Benne's remaining essay, his original short paper at the 1989 Toronto meeting, has been included as the book's prologue.

SOCIAL RECONSTRUCTION THROUGH EDUCATION

What Benne and Stanley, as well as the other contributors in the book have done is examine the connection between educational policy and practice and the ongoing tension between the historically sanctified natural rights of the individual and the needs of the community. This nexus of education, community, and the individual is examined through the historical lens called *social reconstructionism* as each author raises crucial, timely, and critically important questions regarding the role of schools in the 21st century.

Educational reconstructionism, however, is a subject of more than historical interest. Each of the chapters in the book studies the movement as a way of grappling with the critical issue of the relationship between education and social change. We know too little about the progressive and radical alternatives proposed for America's schools during the first half of this century. The economic and social conditions borne from the unchecked growth of 19th-century industrial capitalism ultimately led to the creation of a socially reconstructive school movement during the 1930s. The tensions that existed during the Great Depression—between the promise of plenty and the reality of poverty—are not unlike what we experience today as the culture of postindustrialization shifts to an "information age."

The policy debates and eventually discredited practices of the movement have more or less been ignored by all but a few educational historians and current policy analysts. Taken as a whole, the eight essays analyze the history, philosophy, curricula, and, ultimately, the impact of the left wing of the progressive education movement. Beginning with Benne's first-person account of the genesis of the movement, "Social Reconstructionism Remembered," through Apple's analysis of the conservative ascendancy since the Reagan administration, and then concluding with the Stanley and Benne essay on the promise of a reconstructive community in the 21st century, the book intends to stimulate, broaden, and enrich the legacy of what contributor James Giarelli calls "a public philosophy of education." The volume connects past to present, thus bringing the reader—both educationists and laity—fresh insight into the dilemmas facing schooling in the 1990s, dilemmas more often than not concomitant with the same tensions expressed during the incipient reconstruction debates of the 1930s. Through analysis of social reconstructionism during the 1930s and later decades, the volume will hopefully enrich our understanding of the nexus of school and society. Moreover, explicit within the chapters is the belief that the philosophy and pedagogy undergirding social reconstructionism are alive and well—indeed, in America's present conservative political climate a modern version of reconstructionism is both necessary and possible.

Following Benne's Prologue, the book begins with Apple's "Is Social Transformation Always Progressive? Rightist Reconstructions of Schooling Today." Historically, many have assumed social reconstruction as a progressive or politically left educational ideal. All too often our analysis of social reconstruction assumes that the language of democracy and equality leads in a progressive direction; however, the new right in the United States and Britain has captured much of the language of reconstructionism and has turned the meaning of equality and democracy in a conservative direction. Apple untangles the neoconservative agenda through a framework of reconstructionist tenets and practices, exposing in the process the contradictions of the new right policies and practices that have been consciously situated within the democratic language of the left.

In Giarelli's chapter we move to the founding of the movement, principally to one of the most controversial aspects of depression-era reconstruction, that of *indoctrination for democracy*, an idea at the vortex of educational debate during the 1930s and not without, as Giarelli demonstrates, important consequences for education in the 21st century. Giarelli's analysis of the reconstructionist journal, *The Social Frontier*, examines how the magazine served as a microcosm of many of the problems of the progressive education movement as a whole. Further, he extends this to argue that particular efforts to formulate a radical perspective on American educational problems and solutions reflects the dilemma of modern American radicalism as a whole. The dilemma has been and can be formulated in many ways. How do we preserve the individualistic values of the older community while transforming them into a public ethic more congruent with social, collective, or communal democracy? Is it possible to develop a political state powerful enough to deal with corporate wealth and still prevent that state, with its augmenting power, from being captured by the force we want to control or from becoming repressive itself? It was when this tension was entered into most boldly that *The Social Frontier* was at its best and when it can instruct us most as a philosophical and historical resource in the quest to clarify the most fundamental issues associated with emancipatory and democratic education. Giarelli traces the ways in which this tension was manifested in one of the most important debates in the journal over the question of indoctrination. The debate demanded an explicit confrontation with the dilemmas of freedom and authority, direction and growth, and individual and society, and brought these larger questions to the level of practical educational discourse.

Through *The Social Frontier*, reconstructionists such as George Counts, Harold Rugg, and Theodore Brameld forcefully critiqued school and society in ways that anticipated the critical pedagogy of the 1980s and 1990s. In so doing, the reconstructionists attracted both support and criticism from the leading liberal journals, *The New Republic* and *The Nation*. Wallace's "Red Teachers Can't Save Us: Radical Educators and Liberal Journalists in the 1930s" examines how the relationships among these journals on the left illuminates issues of the 1930s in education, journalism, and politics, and provides perspectives on similar issues in the 1990s.

Of all the leading reconstructionists of the depression decade, Harold Rugg most clearly articulated the connection between ideas and practice. In the chapter, "Harold Rugg's Social Reconstructionism," Carbone and Wilson discuss the theory, practice, and impact of Rugg's career, including his social criticism and recommendations for social change. Rugg was interested in the total reconstruction of American life and his ideas, the authors contend, set him apart from his fellow reconstructionists, many of whom, in Rugg's eyes, tended to limit themselves to economic questions. Rugg's pedagogy was a mix of redemption thorough the arts and social engineering. Carbone and Wilson critique Rugg's most important contribution to social reconstruction and its connection to everyday school practice, his social studies textbooks, and conclude by situating Rugg's version of social reconstruction within current educational debate.

That debate is often centered on how schools should be restructured, including what role traditional bureaucratic hierarchy should play in education for the 21st century. Should leadership be top-down, defined by single individuals, or should schools be governed by an organization of constituencies, grass-roots decision making including faculty, parents, and students. These current issues are not isolated from the past. In "Female Founders and the Progressive Paradox," Semel looks closely at the question of leadership through three case studies of women as founders of independent schools during the progressive era.

As a movement, the study of social reconstruction has been bound by a framework of gender and race. Much of the discussion centers on middle-class white men and the proposed effects of social reconstruction on their communities. During the 1930s, reconstruction was, at least in one state in the South, seized by African-American educators as a potentially powerful democratic tool that might help buttress the African-American community against the ravages of segregation and racism. Using the language of reconstruction—intended by Southern white educators to be the exclusive property of the white community—African-American educators such as Doxie Wilkerson (who would later be vice president of the Communist Party) and Edna Colson (long-time professor of education at Virginia State College) struggled to carve out for the African-American community what James calls "ideological elbow room," that is, increased emphasis on solidarity, knowledge of their African heritage, and an awareness through education in the white community of the rights of African-Americans in a democracy. In the context of pre-civil-rights Southern culture, social reconstruction as envisioned by Wilkerson and the others was truly—and potentially—revolutionary.

Indeed, a democratic society can only flourish through reconstruction. Benne wrote more than 25 years ago in *Education for Tragedy*, that democracy requires:

A leadership which is at once prophetic and therapeutic [and] must work to build and utilize opportunities for developing community of thinking, planning, and action across the lines of entrenched and irrationally defended professional and institutional interests. The stakes of leadership are high. The remaking of collective life in the image of community requires professional leadership, if the fruits and methods of learning and intelligence from research and scholarship are to find their way significantly into personal and collective decisions about our social future. The task of leadership is difficult. Is it too much to believe that members of the teaching profession can come to exercise such leadership? I think not. But the reorientation required within the teaching profession, if such leadership in education collaboration for the building of an educative community is to come to pass, is a major one.[2]

It is in the spirit of that undertaking—the building of a reconstructive, democratic community—that Kenneth went about his life, and in that spirit, this book is dedicated.

---

[2] Kenneth Benne, *Education for Tragedy: Essays in Disenchanted Hope for Modern Man*, (Lexington: University of Kentucky Press, 1967), p. 86.

PROLOGUE: SOCIAL RECONSTRUCTIONISM REMEMBERED

Kenneth D. Benne
Boston University

The discussion of a social movement should perhaps logically begin with an account of its beginning. But, whatever the logic, it is impossible to locate precisely the beginning of any movement in human thought about society and education and about desirable relationships between the two. One might, with some justice, cite Plato's seventh epistle as the origin in Western thought of the idea of changing a society dominated by a tyrant to a meritocratic republic through the agency of education, but its beginning in America is more to the point.

The idea of reconstructing society and culture through the reconstruction of educational institutions, policies, and programs became cogent for more than a few educators in America during the economic depression following the stock market crash in 1929. And a movement, mainly in the education of school teachers and administrators, to advance the idea followed. George Counts and the group that joined him in founding

The Social Frontier: A Journal of Educational Criticism and Reconstruction in 1934 may be thought of as the prophets of the movement in America.

Counts was also the Thomas Paine among early social reconstructionists. He wrote a manifesto, remembered today mainly for its title, *Dare the Schools Build a New Social Order?* He was also the principal author of *A Call to the Teachers of the Nation*, the report of a committee of the Progressive Education Association, which was appointed to study the present and future of school and society during the social, economic, and political crisis of the depression years. In both, he made a telling case that a reconstructed socioeconomic system was required in capitalist America. It was not difficult in the 1930s, with bread lines for hungry people in nearly every city and village, with makeshift shelters for masses of unemployed workers and homeless families, to believe in the abject failure of our economic system. It was especially easy when it was widely publicized that an abundance of economic goods was potential in our means of production and distribution, and that the provision of this abundance to people was being sabotaged by capitalist owners in order to maintain profitability. It was easy also to see grave dangers in the crisis to our political democracy when General MacArthur used soldiers to break up the peaceful encampments of unemployed protesters in Washington, DC during the presidency of Herbert Hoover.

Counts and his social reconstructionist colleagues were deeply committed to the values of democracy, including, but not limited to, political democracy. This commitment has been a constant throughout the history of social reconstructionism. One may quite properly describe the movement as an attempt to deepen and extend the professed democratic commitment of Americans into the planning of economic and social affairs. The social reconstructionists had come to see capitalism, in its late industrial phase, as the foe, not the friend, of democracy. They had also come to see that a little democracy is a dangerous thing insofar as the maintenance of democracy is concerned.

The diagnosis of the historical period that undergirded the prescriptions of the social reconstructionists was succinctly stated by Karl Mannheim, who was something of a social reconstructionist himself in the Europe of that time:

> We are living in an age of transition from *laissez faire* to a planned society. The planned society that will come may take one of two shapes: it will be ruled either by a minority

in terms of a dictatorship or by a new form of government which, in spite of its increased power, will still be democratically controlled.[1]

The need for social and economic planning at local, regional, national and, eventually, world levels was no utopian figment in the imagination of a few left liberal educators in the 1930s, as some contemporary neoconservatives in education would have us believe. This is well illustrated by a question written and published by a distinguished mainstream economist at Columbia University, Wesley C. Mitchell, and a distinguished mainstream political scientist at the University of Chicago, Charles E. Merriam, in 1933. The question appeared in the preface to a multivolume report of a committee on social trends appointed by President Hoover, chaired by Mitchell and Merriam. They were pleading for a planning society in peacetime as well as in wartime. "Is it beyond our human capability," they asked, "to take the enhancement of social welfare as seriously as our generation took the winning of a war?"[2]

The distinctiveness of the social reconstructionists in education was their advocacy of a central role for programs and policies of educational institutions in achieving the deepening and extension of democratic values into the economic and social (ethnic, racial, and social class) relationships through participative planning. This required, among other things, the thorough democratization of our generally autocratic educational institutions.

The principal task of education, as social reconstructionists saw it in the 1930s, was to help build an informed and thoughtful public opinion to support the development of a planning economy geared toward meeting the economic needs of all the people, rather than the maximization of profit for owners of productive property. Fascism, World War II, and the founding of the United Nations led social reconstructionists in the 1940s to add the achievement of world government to the social and political agenda of society and, a fortiori, the agenda of education. This is illustrated by the 1947 decision of the American Education Fellowship, the renamed Progressive Education Association, to

---

[1] Karl Mannheim, *Diagnosis of Our Time* (London: Oxford University Press, 1944), p. 2.

[2] Wesley Mitchell and Charles F. Merriam, *Recent Social Trends in the United States*, (Washington, DC: McGraw-Hill, 1933), VI, p. xxxii.

add world government to domestic social and economic democracy as goals to which the Fellowship was committed. A principal effect of this move, apart from the revivification of the *Progressive Education* magazine, was to split and eventually destroy the Fellowship by the departure of child-centered school devotees from its membership. Of course, McCarthyism and Sputnik played their parts in this result as well.

To the social reconstructionists of the 1930s, technological development was generally regarded as a good thing, undergirding economic plenty for all human beings, if technology was free from the restrictions imposed by a profit-motivated economy. In the late 1940s and the 1950s, the destructive side of unfettered technological development was revealed, not only in the nuclear bomb, but in other threats of a runaway technology to the biosphere as well. This, along with the various liberation movements—racial, sexual, and generational—that emerged in the 1950s and 1960s, led to the following preamble of the latest manifesto by educational reconstructionists in 1968. This was a statement of purposes for the Society for Educational Reconstruction:

> We live in an unprecedented situation. Our world is tormented by widespread poverty, war, the explosion of population, and dehumanizing technological changes. Many contemporary societies have experienced youthful rebellion, insidious or overt forms of racism, and the growing influence of power coalitions such as the military-industrial complex. Urbanization has produced seething misery in our cities. And the schizophrenic, self-imposed splits between reason and feeling, theory and action, means and ends are global in their manifestations. These problems threaten human life. . . . As educators, we believe that our turbulent times require a bold and radically innovative group. For this reason, the Society of Educational Reconstruction (SER) was formed in 1968. This organization commits itself to tapping the potential of education for developing viable ways to resolve humanity's most pressing problems.[3]

---

[3] *The Society for Educational Reconstruction: Statement of Purpose,* (Mimeographed, 1968).

Many members of this Society were contributors to the most comprehensive book-length statement of social reconstructionist treatments of educational theory, policy, and program, edited in 1973 by one of the Society's founding members, Nobuo Shimahara.[4]

The Society for Educational Reconstruction had little influence on the thinking or practice of American educators during the 1970 and 1980s, however accurate their diagnosis of the human condition or however timely and needed their commitments as educators. Philosophy of education, as a discipline, has for the most part become one disciplinary specialization among others. It has avoided the task of clarifying worldwide human problems and of shaping educational efforts toward public understanding of these or commitment toward their melioration. The social foundations movement in teacher education that emerged at the Teachers College of Columbia University in the early 1930s, in parallel with the publication of *The Social Frontier*, did not thrive, as specialized, discipline-centered programs strengthened their hold on teacher education and on schooling generally.

The schools must share responsibility for the widespread economic and political illiteracy that has grown in America, even as the tasks of national and world citizenship have increased in complexity and urgency. I believe we need a new social reconstructionist movement in American education with links to kindred educational movements in other nations. Otherwise, so-called neoconservatives—I prefer the name "reactionaries"—will strengthen their hold on our various institutions of miseducation.

If such a social reconstructionist movement were to be launched among American educators, there are two important lessons to be learned from the failures of the earlier movement. The first has to do with a split that occurred early in the movement and was never fully healed. One branch of the movement, typified by Theodore Bramed, emphasized the need for large and compelling social goals to galvanize and unify educational efforts on behalf of a newer and better society and culture.[5] This

---

[4] Nobuo Shimahara (Ed.), *Educational Reconstruction*, (Columbus, OH: University of Ohio Press, 1973).

[5] See, for example, Theodore Bramed, *Toward a Reconstructed Philosophy of Education*, (New York: Dryden Press, 1956); *The Climactic Decades: Mandate to Education*, (New York: Praeger, 1960).

emphasis, by itself, always raised the specter of "indoctrination" among opponents of a radically reconstructed curriculum and administration in the schools. The second branch is typified by Raup, Benne, Smith, and Axtelle in their work on a discipline of practical judgment.[6] They emphasized the importance of methods of participative planning and deliberation to be focused on value-laden, conflicted human issues. These should become methods of study, action, and evaluation in issue-oriented programs of education. Democratic values must be embodied in the norms of a methodology (scientific method is only a part of such a methodology). These norms must be internalized as a discipline by learners if a planning society is not to also become a centralized tyranny.

Actually, these two emphases in social reconstructionist education need not be in opposition. As issues are studied, goals will emerge. But these must be open to criticism and reconstruction, as well as the means (strategies and tactics) to be employed in attempts to move toward them. An adequate educational methodology of learning and problem solving must incorporate ways of criticizing goals and aims as well as ways of evaluating information and of shaping informed commitments to action.

In the field of curriculum, this bridging between ends and means was begun by Smith, Stanley, and Shores in 1950. They criticized various ways of organizing programs of learning in education and made a powerful case for issue- and problem-centered instruction in a socially reconstructive education.[7] But, as far as I know, later curriculum theorists have not built on these foundations. Subject organization of the curriculum tends to be assumed today, except in scattered "alternative" schools. A new social reconstructionist movement must update and revise Smith, Stanley, and Shores in the field of instruction.

In the field of organization and administration of educational programs, the best social reconstructionist study is still probably that by Jesse Newlon in the 1930s.[8] Newlon sought to relate broad

---

[6] See *Discipline of Practical Judgment in a Democratic Society* (New York: Holt, Rinehart, & Winston, 1943; reprinted as *The Improvement of Practical Intelligence* in 1950 and in 1963). See also Bennis, Benne, and Chin, *The Planning of Change* (4th ed., New York: Holt, Rinehart, & Winston, 1985).

[7] B. Othanel Smith, William O. Stanley, and J. Harlan Shores, *Fundamentals of Curriculum Development*, (New York: World Book Co., 1950).

[8] Jesse Newlon, *Educational Administration as Social Policy*, (New York: C. Scribner's Sons, 1934).

social policy conflicts to the tasks of organizing and administering educational institutions and programs. He saw educational administration as incorporating leadership in changing educational organizations and programs as well as effective management of institutions now established. This emphasis seems to have been lost in later attempts to reduce educational administration to "neutral" organizational management. This is, of course, important, but it involves the common sin among educators of identifying objectivity with neutrality. Most social reconstructionists I have known tried to be objective but they were certainly not neutral.

The second limitation of the social reconstructionist movement in American education has to do with the scope and clientele of a socially reconstructed education. Some of the puzzlement, among those who answered "No" or "Perhaps" to the question posed by Counts' *Dare the Schools Build a New Social Order?*, stemmed from a feeling that children and young people cannot be educated by schools toward radical viewpoints and commitments markedly different from those of their parents and other adults in their society, including the ruling elites. Because most early social reconstructionists were committed to a point of view similar to that of Counts, their movement created a similar puzzlement in many people, even others with radical and left liberal political orientations.

It was not that the social reconstructionists identified education with schooling. They tended rather to identify education with socialization or enculturation and to see schooling as John Dewey expressed the view: "School education is but one educational agency out of many, and at the best is a minor educational force."[9] But the population the social reconstructionists sought directly to reconstruct was the school. They did not deal adequately with the question that sooner or later confronts all advocates of major social and cultural change through educational means: What will we do with unreconstructed adults while we use the education of the "rising generation" as a major instrument in the refashioning of society?

Recall the playful and ironic answer of Socrates to this question in Plato's *Republic*—banish most adults and turn over the direction of the education of the young to philosophers who have somehow seen the light. The sensible answer that has seldom been tried or even advocated by those who see education and re-

---

[9] *The Social Frontier* (May, 1937).

education as centrally necessary ingredients of fundamental social change is to focus reconstructive educational efforts on adults, along with children. Do not neglect the re-education of adults and groups of adults now in positions of major influence in society. I have for a number of years been advocating this notion as one of shifting the focus of educational attention and emphasis from pedagogy to anthropology.[10]

In correctly rejecting the social reconstructionists' advocacy of schools as major agents of social change as "impractical," many educators have, nevertheless, failed to heed and to practice a message for schools that is implicit in that advocacy and that I believe is quite correct and feasible. Boyd Bode expressed this message in dealing with democracy as a way of life, not as a political system of periodic elections of officers: "The school is *par excellence* the institution to which a democratic society is entitled to look for a clarification of the meaning (I would prefer to say the meanings) of democracy."[11] In this failure, schools have not done their bit to meliorate the social and political lives of people caught in the deepening cultural crisis that precipitated the social reconstructionist movement in the first place.

---

[10] Kenneth Benne, "From Pedagogy to Anthropology," Essay 61, In Kenneth D. Benne, *The Task of Post-Contemporary Education* (New York: Teachers College Press, 1990).

[11] Boyd Bode, *Democracy as a Way of Life* (New York: Macmillan, 1937).

1

IS SOCIAL TRANSFORMATION ALWAYS PROGRESSIVE? RIGHTIST RECONSTRUCTIONS OF SCHOOLING TODAY

Michael W. Apple
University of Wisconsin–Madison

INTRODUCTION

The urge to connect schools to a larger social vision, to use them to help reconstruct society, has a long and valuable history in the United States and elsewhere. Although sometimes a bit naïve in their assumptions about the power of our educational institutions in effecting the social transformations that were called for, the more radical elements of movements such as social reconstructionism provided us with a way of envisioning the relationship between schooling and social justice, between schooling, "the people," and a set of norms and values based in equality. Those readers familiar with my own corpus of writing over the past two decades undoubtedly recognize how the roots of much of my work lie in the soil originally tilled by the social reconstructionists.

Even with our critical yet appreciative appraisal of the social reconstructionist impulse, we have tended to assume that most if not all of the attempts to engage schools in larger projects of social transformation are aimed in a progressive direction, that they are aimed toward greater freedom and equality. This is decidedly not the case. In fact, concepts such as freedom and equality are what we might call *sliding signifiers*; their meanings are struggled over, and the role of schooling in society is caught up in the struggles over these meanings. This is exactly what we are witnessing today as the role schools are to play in particular kinds of social transformations is being redefined and as our very concept of democracy is increasingly up for grabs. An understanding of the recent past of right-wing social movements is essential here, because an education that helps reconstruct society so that it is "closer to the people" need not look like that envisioned by many social reconstructionists. The future being constructed may be radical, but may be oddly, though thoroughly, conservative, as well.

THE POLITICIZATION OF EDUCATION

We live in a period in which our educational system has become increasingly politicized. The curriculum and the values that underpin it, and that are included and excluded from it, are now being placed under intense ideological scrutiny. The Spencerian question, "What knowledge is of most worth?" has now been replaced with an even more pointed question: "Whose knowledge is of most worth?" That this latter question has become so powerful highlights the profoundly political nature of educational policy and practice. This is not simply an abstract issue. It is made strikingly clear in the fact that the curriculum of school districts throughout the country has been turned into what can best be described as a political football. Conservative groups in particular have attacked the school and, in the process, have had a major impact on educational debate not only in the United States, but in other nations as well.

As is evident all around us, there has been a significant shift in public discourse around education. The rapid growth of evangelical schooling,[1] the court cases involving "secular humanist" tendencies in textbooks, the increasing attempts to "raise the standards" of teaching and teachers, and the calls in the literature to return to a core curriculum of a common culture all signify a deep suspicion of what is going on in our classrooms among many social groups. There are very real fears—usually among right-wing groups, but also to be found in official statements coming out of the federal and state governments—that for the past decade things have gotten out of control. In this vision, we are losing control both of our children and of the pace of social and cultural change. We have gone too far in tilting our educational and social policies toward minority groups and women. This is not equality, but reverse discrimination; it goes beyond the bounds of what is acceptable. Not only is the search for a more egalitarian set of policies misplaced, but it fails the test of cost–benefit analysis. It is simply too expensive in practice to work and it also gives things to people that they have not really earned.

The position is especially evident in quotes from former Secretary of Education William Bennett. In his view, we are finally emerging out of a crisis in which "we neglected and denied much of the best in American Education. For a period," he wrote, "we simply stopped doing the right things [and] allowed an assault on intellectual and moral standards." This assault on the current state of education, which as previously noted, the conservatives see as being connected with attacks on the family, traditional values, religiosity, patriotism, and our economic well-being, has led schools to fall away from "the principles of our tradition."[2]

Yet, for Bennett, "the people" have now risen up. "The 1980's gave birth to a grass roots movement for educational reform that has generated a renewed commitment to excellence, character, and fundamentals. "Because of this, "we have reason for optimism."[3] Why? Because:

> The national debate on education is now focused on truly important matters: mastering the basics. . . insisting on high standards and expectations; ensuring discipline in the

---

[1] See the excellent discussion in Susan Rose, *Keeping Them Out of the Hands of Satan: Evangelical Schooling in America* (New York: Routledge, 1988).

[2] William J. Bennett, *Our Children and Our Country* (New York: Simon & Schuster, 1988).

[3] Ibid., p. 10.

classroom; conveying a grasp of our moral and political principles; and nurturing the character of our young.[4]

In essence, our educational system has become too committed to a problematic vision of equality. In the process, "our" standards, the cultural and intellectual values of the Western tradition, our very greatness as a nation—and the moral fiber upon which it rests—are at risk. Just as much at risk is our economic stability and our ability to compete internationally in the global market.

All of these points are part of a contradictory bundle of assertions, yet all are having real effects on education and on the lanugage and conceptual apparatus we employ to think about its role in society.

Concepts do not remain still very long. They have wings, so to speak, and can be induced to fly from place to place. It is this context that defines their meaning. As Wittgenstein so nicely reminded us, one should look for the meaning of language in its specific contextual use. This is especially important in understanding political and educational concepts, because they are part of a larger social context, a context that is constantly shifting and is subject to severe ideological conflicts. Education itself is an arena in which these ideological conflicts work themselves out. It is one of the major sites in which different groups with distinct political, economic, and cultural visions attempt to define what the socially legitimate means and ends of a society are to be.

In this chapter, I situate the concern with equality in education within these larger conflicts. I place its shifting meanings both within the breakdown of the largely liberal consensus that guided much educational and social policy after World War II and within the growth of the new right and conservative movements over the past two decades that have had a good deal of success in redefining what education is for and in shifting the ideological texture of the society profoundly to the right.[5] In the process, I document how new social movements gain the ability to redefine—often, though not always in retrogressive ways—the terms

---

[4] Ibid., p. 10.

[5] See Michael W. Apple, *Teachers and Texts: A Political Economy of Class and Gender Relations in Education* (New York: Routledge & Kegan Paul, 1988), and Henry Giroux, "Public Philosophy and the Crisis in Education," *Harvard Educational Review*, 54, (May, 1984), pp. 186–194.

of debate in education, social welfare, and other areas of the common good. At root, my claim is that it is impossible to fully comprehend the value conflicts underlying so much of the debate in education, what has happened to the social reconstructionist project, and the shifting fortunes of the assemblage of concepts surrounding equality (equality of opportunity, equity, etc.) unless we have a much clearer picture of society's already unequal cultural, economic, and political dynamics that provide the center of gravity around which education functions.

BETWEEN PROPERTY RIGHTS AND PERSON RIGHTS

As I have argued at considerably greater length elsewhere, what we are witnessing today is nothing less than the recurrent conflict between *property rights* and *person rights* that has been a central tension in our economy.[6] Gintis defined the differences between property rights and person rights in the following way:

> A property right vests in individuals the power to enter into social relationships on the basis and extent of their property. This may include economic rights of unrestricted use, free contract, and voluntary exchange; political rights of participation and influence; and cultural rights of access to the social means for the transmission of knowledge and the reproduction and transformation of consciousness. A person right vests in individuals the power to enter into these social relationships on the basis of simple membership in the social collectivity. Thus, person rights involve equal treatment of citizens, freedom of expression and movement, equal access to participation in decision-making in social institutions, and reciprocity in relations of power and authority.[7]

---

[6] Michael W. Apple, *Education and Power* (New York: Routledge & Kegan Paul, rev. ARK ed., 1985) and Apple, *Teachers and Texts*.

[7] Herbert Gintis, "Communication and Politics," *Socialist Review*, 10 (March–June 1980), p. 193.

The attempts to enhance person rights partly rest on a notion of what is best thought of as positive liberty, "freedom to" as well as "freedom from." In industrial nations, this has grown stronger over the years as many previously disenfranchised groups demanded suffrage. The right to equal political participation would be based on being a person rather than on ownership of property (or later on being a White male). Further, person rights have been extended to include the right of paid workers to form unions to organize a common front against their employers. At the same time, claims about the right to have a job with dignity and decent pay have been advanced. And, finally, there have been demands that economic transactions—from equal treatment of women and people of color in employment, pay, and benefits, to health and safety for everyone—are to be governed by rules of due process and fairness, thereby restricting management powers of unrestricted use and "free contract."[8]

This last point is important because it documents a growing tendency to take ideas of civil equality and apply them to the economic sphere. Thus, "the right to equal treatment in economic relationships, which directly expresses the dominance of person over property rights, has been an explicit demand of women, racial minorities, immigrant workers, and others."[9] This, too, has been accompanied by further gains in which the positive rights of suffrage and association that have been won by women and by minority and working-class groups have been extended to include what increasingly became seen as a set of minimum rights due any individual simply by the fact of citizenship. These included state-supported services in the areas of health, education, and social security, consumer protection laws, lifeline utility guarantees, and occupational safety and health regulations. In their most progressive moments, these tendencies led to arguments for full workplace democracy, democratic control over investment decisions, and the extension of the norms of reciprocity and mutual participation and control in most areas of social life, from the paid workplace and the political life of local communities and schools to the home.[10] Taken together, these movements did constitute at least a partial restructuring of the balance between person rights and property rights, one that would soon be challenged by powerful groups.

---

[8] Ibid., p. 196.
[9] Ibid., p. 197.
[10] Ibid., p. 197.

It is not surprising that in our society dominant groups "have fairly consistently defended the prerogatives of property," whereas subordinate groups on the whole have sought to advance "the prerogatives of persons."[11] In times of severe upheaval, these conflicts become even more intense and, given the current balance of power in society, advocates of property rights have once again been able to advance their claims for the restoration and expansion of their prerogatives not only in education, but in all of our social institutions.

The U. S. economy is in the midst of one of the most powerful structural crises it has experienced since the depression. In order to solve it on terms acceptable to dominant interests, as many aspects of society as possible need to be pressured into conforming with the requirements of international competition, reindustrialization, and (in the words of the National Commission on Excellence in Education) "rearmament." The gains made in employment, health and safety, welfare programs, affirmative action, legal rights, and education must be rescinded because they are too expensive both economically and ideologically.

Both of these latter words are important. Not only are fiscal resources scarce (in part because current policies transfer them to the military), but people must be convinced that their belief that person rights come first is simply wrong or outmoded given current realities. Thus, intense pressure must be brought to bear through legislation, persuasion, administrative rules, and ideological maneuvering to create the conditions right-wing groups believe are necessary to meet these requirements.[12]

In the process, in Britain and Australia as well as in the United States, the emphasis of public policy has materially changed from issues of employing the state to overcome disadvantage. Equality, no matter how limited or broadly conceived, has been redefined. No longer is it linked to past *group* oppression and disadvantagement. It is simply now a case of guaranteeing *individual choice* under the conditions of a "free market."[13] Thus, the current emphasis on "excellence" (a word with multiple meanings and social uses) has shifted educational discourse so

---

[11] Ibid., p. 194. See also Samuel Bowles and Herbert Gintis, *Democracy and Capitalism* (New York: Basic Books, 1986).

[12] Apple, *Teachers and Texts*.

[13] Mary Anderson, *Teachers Unions and Industrial Politics*, Unpublished doctoral dissertation (School of Behavioral Science, Macquarie University, Sydney, Australia, 1985), pp. 6–8.

8 MICHAEL W. APPLE

that underachievement is once again increasingly seen as largely the fault of the student. Student failure, which was at least partly interpreted as the fault of severely deficient educational policies and practices, is now seen as the result of what might be called the biological and economic marketplace. This is evidenced in the growth of forms of Social Darwinist thinking in education and in public policy in general.[14] In a similar way, behind a good deal of the rhetorical artifice of concern about the achievement levels in, say, inner-city schools, notions of choice have begun to evolve in which deep-seated school problems will be solved by establishing free competition over students. These assume that by expanding the capitalist marketplace to schools, we will somehow compensate for the decades of economic and educational neglect experienced by the communities in which these schools are found.[15] Finally, there are concerted attacks on teachers (and curricula) based on a profound mistrust of their quality and commitments.

All of this has led to an array of educational conflicts that have been instrumental in shifting the debates over education profoundly to the right. The effects of this shift can be seen in a number of educational policies and proposals now gaining momentum throughout the country: (a) proposals for voucher plans and tax credits to make schools more like the idealized free market economy; (b) the movement in state legislatures and state departments of education to raise standards and mandate both teacher and student competencies and basic curricular goals and knowledge, thereby centralizing even more at a state level the control of teaching and curricula; (c) the increasingly effective assaults on the school curriculum for its supposedly antifamily and anti-free-enterprise bias, its secular humanism, its lack of patriotism, and its neglect of the Western tradition; and (d) the growing pressure to make the needs of business and industry into the primary goals of the educational system.[16] These are major alterations, ones that have taken years to show their effects. Although I paint in rather broad strokes here, an outline of the social and ideological dynamics of how this has occurred should be visible.

---

[14] Ann Bastian, Norm Fruchter, Marilyn Gittell, Colin Greer, and Kenneth Haskins, *Choosing Equality: The Case for Democratic Schooling* (Philadelphia: Temple University Press, 1986), p. 14.

[15] I wish to thank my colleague Walter Secada for this point.

[16] See Apple, *Teachers and Texts*.

THE RESTORATION POLITICS
OF AUTHORITARIAN POPULISM

The first thing to ask about an ideology is not what is false about it, but what is true. What are its connections to lived experience? Ideologies, properly conceived, do not dupe people. To be effective they must connect to real problems and real experiences.[17] As I document, the movement away from social democratic principles and an acceptance of more right-wing positions in social and educational policy occur precisely because conservative groups have been able to work on popular sentiments, to reorganize genuine feelings, and in the process to win adherents.

Important ideological shifts take place, but not only in powerful groups "substituting one, whole, new conception of the world for another." Often, these shifts occur through the presentation of novel combinations of old and new elements.[18] Let us take the positions of the Reagan administration, ones which by and large provided the framework for the Bush administration's policies as well, as a case in point; for as Clark and Astuto have demonstrated in education and Piven and Cloward and Raskin have shown in the larger areas of social policy, significant and enduring alterations have occurred in the ways policies are carried out and in the content of those policies.[19]

The success of the policies of the Reagan administration, like that of Thatcherism in Britain, should not simply be evaluated

---

[17] See Michael W. Apple, *Ideology and Curriculum* (New York: Routledge, rev. ed., 1990) and Jorge Larrain, *Marxism and Ideology* (Atlantic Highlands, NJ: Humanities Press, 1983).

[18] Stuart Hall, "Authoritarian Populism: A Reply," *New Left Review*, 151, (May–June 1985), p. 122.

[19] David Clark and Terry Astuto, "The Significance and Permanence of Changes in Federal Education Policy," *Educational Researcher*, 15 (October 1986), pp. 4–13; Frances Piven and Richard Cloward, *The New Class War* (New York: Pantheon, 1982); Marcus Raskin, *The Common Good* (New York: Routledge & Kegan Paul, 1986). Clark and Astuto point out that during Reagan's terms, the following initiatives characterized educational policies: reducing the federal role in education, stimulating competition among schools with the aim of "breaking the monopoly of the public school," fostering individual competition so that "excellence" is gained, increasing the reliance on performance standards for students and teachers, an emphasis on the "basics" in content, increasing parental choice "over what, where, and how their children learn," strengthening the teaching of "traditional values" in schools, and expanding the policy of transferring educational authority to the state and local levels (p. 8).

in electoral terms. They need to also be judged by their success in disorganizing other more progressive groups and in shifting the terms of political, economic, and cultural debate onto the terrain favored by capital and the right.[20] In these terms, there can be no doubt that the current right-wing resurgence has accomplished no small amount in its attempt to construct the conditions that will put it in a hegemonic position.

The right in the United States and Britain has thoroughly renovated and reformed itself. It has developed strategies based upon what might best be called an *authoritarian populism*.[21] As Hall defined this, such a policy is based on an increasingly close relationship between government and the capitalist economy, a radical decline in the institutions and power of political democracy, and attempts at curtailing liberties that have been gained in the past. This is coupled with attempts to build a widespread consensus in support of these actions.[22] The new right's authoritarian populism[23] has exceptionally long roots in the history of the United States. The political culture here has always been influenced by the values of the dissenting Protestantism of the 17th century. Such roots become even more evident in periods of intense social change and crisis.[24] As Burnham put it:

> Whenever and wherever the pressures of "modernization"—secularity, urbanization, the growing importance of science—have become unusually intense, episodes of revivalism and culture-issue politics have swept over the social landscape. In all such cases since at least the end of the Civil

---

[20] Stuart Hall and Martin Jacques, "Introduction," In Stuart Hall and Martin Jacques (Eds.), *The Politics of Thatcherism* (London: Lawrence & Wishart, 1983), p. 13.

[21] Stuart Hall, "Popular Democratic vs. Authoritarian Populism: Two Ways of Taking Democracy Seriously," In Alan Hunt (Ed.), *Marxism and Democracy* (London: Lawrence & Wishart, 1980), pp. 160–161.

[22] Ibid., p. 161.

[23] I realize that there is debate over the adequacy of this term. See Hall, "Authoritarian Populism: A Reply" and B. Jessop, K. Bennett, S. Bromley, and T. Ling, "Authoritarian Populism, Two Nations, and Thatcherism," *New Left Review*, 147 (1984), pp. 33–60. *Authoritarian populism* is, of course, a term that denotes a central tendency of a broad and varied movement, as I show later on in my discussion.

[24] Michael Omi and Howard Winant, *Racial Formation in the United States* (New York: Routledge & Kegan Paul, 1986), p. 214.

War, such movements have been more or less explicitly reactionary, and have frequently been linked with other kinds of reaction in explicitly political ways.[25]

The new right works on these roots in creative ways, modernizing them and creating a new synthesis of their varied elements by linking them to current fears. In so doing, the right has been able to rearticulate traditional political and cultural themes, effectively mobilizing a large amount of mass support.

As I noted, part of the strategy has been the attempted dismantling of the welfare state and of the benefits that working people, people of color, and women (these categories are obviously not mutually exclusive) have won over decades of hard work. This has been done under the guise of antistatism, of keeping government "off the backs of the people," and of "free enterprise." Yet, at the same time, in many valuative, political, and economic areas, the current government is extremely state centrist both in its outlook, and very importantly in its day-to-day operations.[26]

One of the major aims of a rightist restoration politics is to struggle in not one but many different arenas at the same time; not only in the economic sphere, but also in education and elsewhere. This aim is grounded in the realization that economic dominance must be coupled to political, moral, and intellectual leadership if a group is to be truly dominant and if it wants to genuinely restructure a social formation. Thus, as both Reaganism and Thatcherism recognized so clearly, to win in the state you must also win in civil society.[27] As noted Italian political theorist Antonio Gramsci put it, what we are seeing is a war of position: "It takes place where the whole relation of the state to civil society, to 'the people' and to popular struggles, to the individual and to the economic life of society has been thoroughly reorganized, where 'all the elements change'."[28]

In this restructuring, Reaganism and Thatcherism did not create some sort of false consciousness, creating ways of seeing that had little connection with reality. Rather, they "operated directly on the real and manifestly contradictory experiences" of a large portion of the population. They did connect with the

---

[25] Walter Dean Burnham, "Post-conservative America," *Socialist Review*, 13 (November–December 1983), p. 125.
[26] Hall, "Authoritarian Populism: A Reply," p. 117.
[27] Ibid., p. 112.
[28] Hall, "Popular Democratic and Authoritarian Populism," p. 166.

perceived needs, fears, and hopes of groups of people who felt threatened by the range of problems associated with the crises in authority relations, the economy, and politics.[29]

What has been accomplished is a successful translation of an economic doctrine into the language of experience, moral imperative, and common sense. The free market ethic has been combined with a populist politics. This has meant the blending together of a "rich mix" of themes that have had a long history—nation, family, duty, authority, standards, and traditionalism—with other thematic elements that have also struck a resonant chord during a time of crisis. These latter themes include self-interest, competitive individualism (what I have elsewhere called the possessive individual),[30] and antistatism. In this way, a reactionary common sense is partly created.[31]

The sphere of education has been one of the most successful areas for the right. The social democratic goal of expanding equality of opportunity (itself a rather limited reform) has lost much of its political potency and its ability to mobilize people. The panic over falling standards and illiteracy, fears of violence in schools, and concern with the destruction of family values and religiosity have all had an effect. These fears are exacerbated and used by dominant groups within politics and the economy, who have been able to move the debate on education (and all things social) onto their own terrain—the terrain of traditionalism, standardization, productivity, and industrial needs.[32] Because so many parents are justifiably concerned about the economic futures of their children—in an economy that is increasingly conditioned by lowered wages, unemployment, capital flight, and insecurity[33]—rightist discourse connects with the experiences of many working-class and lower middle-class people.

However, as this conservative conceptual and ideological apparatus appears to be rapidly gaining ground, one of the most

---

[29] Stuart Hall, "The Great Moving Right Show," In Stuart Hall and Martin Jacques (Eds.), *The Politics of Thatcherism*.

[30] Apple, *Education and Power*.

[31] Hall, "The Great Moving Right Show," pp. 29–30.

[32] Ibid., pp. 36–37. For an illuminating picture of how these issues are manipulated by powerful groups, see Allen Hunter, *Virtue With a Vengeance: The Pro-Family Politics of The New Right*, Unpublished doctoral dissertation, (Department of Sociology, Brandeis University, Waltham, MA, 1984).

[33] See Apple, *Teachers and Texts*.

critical issues remains to be answered. How *is* such an ideological vision legitimated and accepted? How was this done?[34]

UNDERSTANDING THE CRISIS

The right-wing resurgence is not simply a reflection of the current crisis; rather, it is a response to that crisis.[35] Beginning in the immediate post-World War II years, the political culture of the United States was increasingly characterized by American imperial might, economic affluence, and cultural optimism. This period lasted for more than two decades. Socially and politically, it was a time of what has been called the *social democratic accord*, in which government increasingly became an arena for a focus on the conditions required for equality of opportunity. Commodity-driven prosperity, the extension of rights and liberties to new groups, and the expansion of welfare provisions provided the conditions for this compromise both between capital and labor and with historically more dispossessed groups such as African-Americans and women. This accord has become mired in crisis since the late 1960s and early 1970s.[36]

Allen Hunter gave an excellent sense of this in his own description of this accord:

> From the end of World War II until the early 1970s world capitalism experienced the longest period of sustained economic growth in its history. In the United states a new "social structure of accumulation"—"the specific institutional environment within which the capitalist accumulation process is organized"—was articulated around several prominent features: the broadly shared goal of sustained economic growth, Keynesianism, elite pluralist democracy, an imperial America prosecuting a cold war, anti-communism at home and abroad, stability or incremental change

---

[34] Jessop, Bennett, Bromley, and Ling, "Authoritarian Populism, Two Nations, and Thatcherism," p. 49.

[35] Hall, "The Great Moving Right Show," p. 21.

[36] Allen Hunter, "The Politics of Resentment and the Construction of Middle America," Unpublished paper (American Institutions Program, University of Wisconsin, Madison, 1987), pp. 1-3.

in race relations and a stable home life in a buoyant, commodity-driven consumer culture. Together these crystallized a basic consensus and a set of social and political institutions which was hegemonic for two decades.[37]

At the very center of this hegemonic accord was a compromise reached between capital and labor in which labor accepted what might be called "the logic of profitability and markets as the guiding principles of resource allocation." In return they received "an assurance that minimal living standards, trade union rights and liberal democratic rights would be protected."[38] These democratic rights were further extended to the poor, women, and people of color as these groups expanded their own struggles to overcome racial and sexual discriminatory practices.[39] Yet, this extension of (limited) rights could not last, given the economic and ideological crises that soon beset American society, a set of crises that challenged the very core of the social democratic accord.

The dislocations of the 1960s and 1970s—the struggle for racial and sexual equality, military adventures such as Vietnam, Watergate, and the resilience of the economic crisis—produced both shock and fear. Mainstream culture was shaken to its very roots in many ways. Widely shared notions of family, community, and nation were dramatically altered. Just as importantly, no new principle of cohesion emerged that was sufficiently compelling to re-create a cultural center. As economic, political, and valuative stability (and military supremacy) seemed to disappear, the polity was itself "balkanized." Social movements based on difference—regional, racial, sexual, and religious— became more visible.[40] The sense of what Marcus Raskin called "the common good" was fractured.[41]

Traditional social democratic "statist" solutions, which in education, welfare, health, and other similar areas took the form of large-scale attempts at federal intervention, to increase opportunities or to provide a minimal level of support were seen as

---

[37] Ibid., p. 9.

[38] Samuel Bowles, "The Post-Keynesian Capital Labor Stalemate," *Socialist Review*, 12 (September–October 1982), p. 51.

[39] Hunter, "The Politics of Resentment and the Construction of Middle America," p. 12.

[40] Omi and Winant, *Racial Formation in the United States*, pp. 214–215.

[41] Raskin, *The Common Good*.

being part of the problem not as part of the solution. Traditional conservative positions were more easily dismissed as well. After all, the society on which they were based was clearly being altered. The cultural center could be *built* (and it had to be built by well-funded and well-organized political and cultural action) around the principles of the new right. The new right confronts the "moral, existential, [and economic] chaos of the preceding decades" with a network of exceedingly well-organized and financially secure organizations incorporating "an aggressive political style, on outspoken religious and cultural traditionalism and a clear populist commitment."[42]

In different words, the project was aimed at constructing a "new majority" that would "dismantle the welfare state, legislate a return to traditional morality, and stem the tide of political and cultural dislocation which the 1960's and 1970's represented." Using a populist political strategy (now in combination with an aggressive executive branch of the government), it marshaled an assault on "liberalism and secular humanism" and linked that assault to what some observers have argued was "an obsession with individual guilt and responsibility where social questions are concerned (crime, sex, education, poverty)" with strong beliefs against government intervention.[43]

The class, racial, and sexual specificities here are significant. The movement to create a conservative cultural consensus in part builds on the hostilities of the working- and lower middle classes toward those above and below them and is also fueled by a very real sense of antagonism against the new middle class. State bureaucrats and administrators, educators, journalists, planners, and so on all share part of the blame for the social dislocations these groups have experienced.[44] Race, gender, and class

---

[42] Omi and Winant, *Racial Formation in the United States*, pp. 215–216. See also Hunter, *Virtue With a Vengeance*.

[43] Omi and Winant, *Racial Formation in the United States*, p. 220. For a more complete discussion of how this has affected educational policy in particular, see Clark and Astuto, "The Significance and Permanence of Changes in Federal Education Policy," and Apple, *Teachers and Texts*.

[44] Omi and Winant, *Racial Formation in the United States*, p. 221. I have elsewhere claimed, and point out later, however, that some members of the new middle class—namely efficiency experts, evaluators and testers, and many of those with technical and management expertise—will form part of the alliance with the new right. This is simply because their own jobs and mobility depend on it. See Apple, *Teachers and Texts* and Michael W. Apple, "Education, Culture and Class Power," *Educational Theory*, 42, (Spring 1992), pp. 127–145.

themes abound, a point to which I return in the next section of my analysis.

This movement is of course enhanced within academic and government circles by a group of policy-oriented neoconservatives who have become the organic intellectuals for much of the rightist resurgence. A society based on individualism, market-based opportunities, and the drastic reduction of both state intervention and state support run deep in their work.[45] They provide a counterpart to the new right and are themselves part of the inherently unstable alliance that has been formed.

BUILDING THE NEW ACCORD

Almost all of the reform-minded social movements—including the feminist, gay and lesbian, student, and other movements of the 1960s—drew on the struggle by African-Americans "as a central organizational fact or as a defining political metaphor and inspiration."[46] These social movements infused new social meanings into politics, economics, and culture. These are not separate spheres; all three of these levels exist simultaneously. New social meanings about the importance of person rights infused individual identity, family, and community, and penetrated state institutions and market relationships. These emerging social movements expanded the concerns of politics to all aspects of the "terrain of everyday life." Person rights took on even more importance in nearly all of our institutions, as evidenced in aggressive affirmative action programs, widespread welfare and educational activist programs, and so on.[47] In education this was very clear in the growth of bilingual programs

---

[45] Omi and Winant, *Racial Formation in the United States*, p. 227.

[46] Ibid., p. 164.

[47] Ibid., p. 164. See also Samuel Bowles and Herbert Gintis, *Democracy and Capitalism*. The discussion in Bowles and Gintis of the "transportability" of struggles over person rights from, say, politics to the economy is very useful here. I have extended and criticized some of their claims in Michael W. Apple, "Facing the Complexity of Power: For a Parallelist Position in Critical Educational Studies," In Mike Cole (Ed.), *Rethinking Bowles and Gintis* (Philadelphia: Falmer Press, 1988).

and in the development of women's, African-American, Hispanic, and Native American studies in high schools and colleges.

There are a number of reasons the state was the chief target of these earlier social movements for gaining person rights. First, the state was the "factor of cohesion in society" and had historically maintained and organized practices and policies that embodied the tension between property rights and person rights.[48] As such a factor of cohesion, it was natural to focus on it. Second, "the state was traversed by the same antagonisms which penetrated the larger society, antagonisms that were themselves the results of past cycles of [social] struggle." Openings in the state could be gained because of this. Footholds in state institutions dealing with education and social services could be deepened.[49]

Yet even with these gains, the earlier coalitions began to disintegrate. In communities of color, class polarization deepened. The majority of barrio and ghetto residents "remained locked in poverty," although a relatively small portion of the population was able to take advantage of educational opportunities and new jobs (the latter being largely within the state itself).[50] With the emerging crisis in the economy, something of a zero-sum game developed in which progressive social movements had to fight over a limited share of resources and power. Antagonistic rather than complementary relationships developed among groups. Minority groups, for example, and the largely White middle-class women's movement had difficulty integrating their programs, goals, and strategies.

This was exacerbated by the fact that, unfortunately, given the construction of a zero-sum game by dominant groups, the gains made by women sometimes came at the expense of other minorities. Furthermore, leaders of many of these movements had been absorbed into state-sponsored programs which—although the adoption of such programs was in part a victory—had the latent affect of cutting off leaders from their grass-roots constituency and lessening the militancy at this level. This often resulted in what was called the *ghettoization* of movements within state institutions as movement demands were partly adopted in their

---

[48] See Apple, *Education and Power* and *Teachers and Texts*.

[49] Omi and Winant, *Racial Formation in the United States*, pp. 177–178.

[50] Ibid., pp. 177–178.

most moderate forms into programs sponsored by the state. Militancy is transformed into constituency.[51]

The splits in these movements occurred also because of strategic divisions that were paradoxically the results of the movements' own successes. Thus, for example, those women who aimed their work within existing political and economic channels could point to gains in employment within the state and in the economic sphere. Other, more radical, members saw such "progress" as 'too little, too late."[52]

Nowhere is this more apparent than in the African-American movement in the United States. It is worth quoting one of the best analyses of the history of these divisions at length:

> The movement's limits also arose from the strategic divisions that befell it as a result of its own successes. Here the black movement's fate is illustrative. Only in the South, while fighting against a backward political structure and overt cultural oppression, had the black movement been able to maintain a *de*-centered unity, even when internal debates were fierce. Once it moved north, the black movement began to split, because competing political projects, linked to different segments of the community, sought either integration in the (reformed) mainstream, or more radical transformation of the dominant racial order.
>
> After initial victories against segregation were won, one sector of the movement was thus reconstituted as an interest-group, seeking an end to racism understood as discrimination and prejudice, and turning its back on the oppositional "politics of identity." Once the organized black movement became a mere constituency, though, it found itself locked in a bear hug with the state institutions whose programs it had itself demanded, while simultaneously isolated from the core institutions of the modern state.[53]

In the process, those sectors of the movement that were the most radical were marginalized or, and this must not be forgotten, were simply repressed by the state.[54]

---

[51] Ibid., p. 180.
[52] Ibid., p. 180.
[53] Ibid., p. 190.
[54] Ibid., p. 190.

Even though there were major gains, the movements' integration into the state latently created conditions that were disastrous in the fight for equality. A mass-based militant grass-roots movement was defused into a constituency, dependent on the state itself. When the neoconservative and right-wing movements evolved with their decidedly antistatist themes, the gains that were made in the state came increasingly under attack and the ability to re-create a large-scale grass-roots movement to defend these gains was weakened considerably.[55] Thus, when there are right-wing attacks on the more progressive national and local educational policies and practices that have benefited people of color, it becomes increasingly difficult to develop broad-based coalitions to counter these offensives.

In their failure to consolidate a new "radical" democratic politics, one with majoritarian aspirations, the new social movements of the 1960s and 1970s "provided the political space in which right wing reaction could incubate and develop its political agenda."[56] Thus, state reforms won by, say, minority movements in the 1960s in the United States, and the new definitions of person rights embodied in these reforms, "provided a formidable range of targets for the 'counter-reformers' of the 1970s." Neoconservatives and the new right carried on their own political "project." They were able to rearticulate particular ideological themes and to restructure them around a political movement once again.[57] And these themes *were* linked to the dreams, hopes, and fears of many individuals.

Let us examine this in somewhat more detail. Behind the conservative restoration and reconstruction is a clear sense of loss: of control, economic and personal security, the knowledge and values that should be passed on to children, and visions of what counts as sacred texts and authority. The binary opposition of we/they becomes very important here. *We* are law abiding, "hard working, decent, virtuous, and homogeneous." The *theys* are very different. They are "lazy, immoral, permissive, heterogenous."[58] These binary oppositions distance most people of color, women, gays, and others from the community of worthy individuals. The subjects of discrimination are now no longer

---

[55] Ibid., p. 190.
[56] Ibid., p. 252.
[57] Ibid., p. 155.
[58] Hunter, "The Politics of Resentment and the Construction of Middle America," p. 23.

those groups who have been historically oppressed, but are instead the "real Americans" who embody the idealized virtues of a romanticized past. The theys are undeserving. They are getting something for nothing. Policies supporting them are "sapping our way of life," most of our economic resources, and creating government control of our lives.[59]

These processes of ideological distancing make it possible for anti-African-American and antifeminist sentiments to seem no longer racist and sexist because they link so closely with other issues. Once again, Allen Hunter is helpful:

> Racial rhetoric links with anti-welfare state sentiments, fits with the push for economic individualism; thus many voters who say they are not prejudiced (and may not be by some accounts) oppose welfare spending as unjust. Antifeminist rhetoric..is articulated around defense of the family, traditional morality, and religious fundamentalism.[60]

All of these elements can be integrated through the formation of ideological coalitions that enable many Americans, who themselves feel under threat, to turn against groups of people who are even less powerful than themselves. At the very same time, it enables them to "attack domination by liberal, statist elites."[61]

This ability to identify a range of "others" as enemies, as the source of the problems, is very significant. One of the major elements in this ideological formation has been a belief that liberal elites within the state "were intruding themselves into home life, trying to impose their values." This was having serious negative effects on moral values and on traditional families. Much of the conservative criticism of textbooks and curricula rests on these feelings, for example. Although this position certainly exaggerated the impact of the liberal elite, and although it certainly misrecognized the power of capital and of other dominant classes,[62] there was enough of an element of truth in it for the right to use it in its attempts to dismantle the previous accord and build its own.

---

[59] Ibid., p. 30.
[60] Ibid., p. 33.
[61] Ibid., p. 34.
[62] Ibid., p. 21.

A new hegemonic accord is reached, then. It combines dominant economic and political elites intent on "modernizing" the economy, white working-class and middle-class groups concerned with security, the family, and traditional knowledge and values, and economic conservatives.[63] It also includes a fraction of the new middle class, whose own advancement depends on the expanded use of accountability, efficiency, and management procedures, which are their own cultural capital.[64] This coalition has partly succeeded in altering the very meaning of what it means to have a social goal of equality. The citizen as "free" consumer has replaced the previously emerging citizen as situated in structurally generated relations of domination. Thus, the common good is now to be regulated exclusively by the laws of the market, free competition, private ownership, and profitability. In essence, the definitions of freedom and equality are no longer democratic, but *commercial*.[65] This is particularly evident in the proposals for voucher plans as solutions to massive and historically rooted relations of economic and cultural inequality.

WILL THE RIGHT SUCCEED?

So far I have broadly traced out many of the political, economic, and ideological reasons that the social democratic consensus that led to the limited extension of person rights in education, politics, and the economy slowly disintegrated. At the same time, I have documented how a new hegemonic bloc is being formed, coalescing around new right tactics and principles. The question remains: Will this accord be long lasting? Will it be able to inscribe its principles into the very heart of the American polity?

There are very real obstacles to the total consolidation within the state of the new right political agenda. First, there has been

---

[63] Ibid., p. 37.

[64] Apple, *Teachers and Texts;* Basil Bernstein, *The Structuring of Pedagogic Discourse* (New York: Routledge, 1990).

[65] Stuart Hall, "Popular Culture and the State," in Tony Bennett, Colin Mercer, and Janet Woollacott (Eds.), *Popular Culture and Social Relations* (Milton Keynes, England: Open University Press, 1986), pp. 35–36.

something of a "great transformation" in, say, racial identities. Omi and Winant described it:

> The forging of new collective racial identities during the 1950s and 1960s has been the enduring legacy of the racial minority movements. Today, as gains won in the past are rolled back and most organizations prove unable to rally a mass constituency in racial minority communities, the persistence of the new racial identities developed during this period stands out as the single truly formidable obstacle to the consolidation of a newly repressive racial order.[66]

Thus, even when social movements and political coalitions are fractured, when their leaders are coopted, repressed, and sometimes killed, the racial subjectivity and self-awareness that were developed by these movements has taken permanent hold. "No amount of repression or cooptation [can] change that."[67] In Omi and Winant's words, the genie is out of the bottle.[68] This is the case because, in essence, a new kind of person has been created within minority communities.[69] A new, and much more self-conscious, *collective* identity has been forged. Thus, for instance, in the struggles over the past three decades by people of color to have more control of education and to have it respond more directly to their own culture and collective histories, these people themselves were transformed in major ways.[70] Thus:

> Social movements create collective identity by offering their adherents a different view of themselves and their world; different, that is, from the world view and self-concepts offered by the established social order. They do this by the process of *rearticulation*, which produces new subjectivity by making use of information and knowledge already

---

[66] Omi and Winant, *Racial Formation in the United States*, p. 165.

[67] Ibid., p. 166.

[68] Ibid., p. 166.

[69] I say "new" here, but the continuity of, say, African-American struggles for freedom and equality also needs to be stressed. See the powerful treatment of the history of such struggles in Vincent Harding, *There is a River: The Black Struggle for Freedom in the United States* (New York: Vintage Books, 1981).

[70] See also David Hogan, "Education and Class Formation," In Michael W. Apple, *Cultural and Economic Reproduction in Education* (Boston: Routledge & Kegan Paul, 1982), pp. 32–78.

present in the subject's mind. They take elements and themes of her/his culture and traditions and infuse them with new meaning.[71]

These meanings will make it exceedingly difficult for the right to incorporate the perspectives of people of color under its ideological umbrella and will continually create oppositional tendencies within the African-American community. The slow but steady growth in the power of people of color at a local level in these communities will serve as a countervailing force to the solidification of the new conservative accord.

Added to this is the fact that even within the new hegemonic bloc, even within the conservative restoration coalition, there are ideological strains that may have serious repercussions on its ability to be dominant for an extended period. These tensions are partly generated because of the class dynamics within the coalition. Fragile compromises may come apart because of the sometimes directly contradictory beliefs held by many of the partners in the new accord.

This can be seen in the example of two of the groups now involved in supporting the accord. There are both what can be called residual and emergent ideological systems or codes at work here. The residual culture and ideologies of the old middle class and of an upwardly mobile portion of the working class and lower middle class—stressing control, individual achievement, "morality," and so on—has been merged with the emergent code of a portion of the new middle class—getting ahead, technique, efficiency, bureaucratic advancement, and so on.[72]

These codes are in an inherently unstable relationship. The stress on new right morality does not necessarily sit well with an amoral emphasis on careerism and economic norms. The merging of these codes can only last as long as paths to mobility are not blocked. The economy must pay off in jobs and mobility for the new middle class or the coalition is threatened. There is no guarantee, given the unstable nature of the economy and the kinds of jobs being created, that this pay off will occur.[73]

This tension can be seen in another way that shows again that, in the long run, the prospects for such a lasting ideological coalition are not necessarily good. Under the new, more conservative

---

[71] Omi and Winant, *Racial Formation in the United States*, p. 166.
[72] See Apple, *Teachers and Texts*.
[73] See Apple, *Teachers and Texts*.

accord, the conditions for capital accumulation and profit must be enhanced by state activity as much as possible; thus, the "free market" must be set loose. As many areas of public and private life as possible need to be brought into line with such privatized market principles, including the schools, health care, welfare, housing, and so on. Yet, in order to create profit, capitalism also requires that traditional values are subverted. Commodity purchasing and market relations become the norm and older values of community, "sacred knowledge," and morality will need to be cast aside. This dynamic sets in motion the seeds of possible conflicts in the future between the economic modernizers and the new right cultural traditionalists who make up a significant part of the coalition that has been built.[74] Furthermore, the competitive individualism now being so heavily promoted in educational reform movements in the United States may not respond well to traditional working-class and poor groups' somewhat more collective senses.

Finally, there are counterhegemonic movements now being built within education itself. The older social democratic accord included many educators, union leaders, minority group members, and others. There are signs that the fracturing of this coalition may only be temporary. Take teachers, for instance. Even though salaries have been on the rise throughout the country, this has been countered by a rapid increase in the external control of teachers' work, the rationalization and deskilling of their jobs, and the growing blame of teachers and education in general for most of the major social ills that beset the economy.[75] Many teachers have organized around these issues, in a manner reminiscent of the earlier work of the Boston Women's Teachers' Group.[76] Furthermore, there are signs throughout the country of multiracial coalitions being built among elementary and secondary school teachers, university-based educators, and community members to collectively act on the conditions under which teachers work and to support the democratization of curriculum and teaching and a rededication to the equalization of

---

[74] See Apple, *Teachers and Texts*. For a comprehensive analysis of the logic of capitalism that compares it with other political and economic traditions, see Andrew Levine, *Arguing for Socialism* (Boston: Routledge & Kegan Paul, 1984).

[75] See Apple, *Education and Power*, and *Teachers and Texts*.

[76] See Sara Freedman, Jane Jackson, and Katherine Boles, *The Effects of the Institutional Structure of Schools on Teachers* (Somerville, MA: Boston Women's Teachers' Group, 1982).

access and outcomes in schooling. The Southern Coalition for Educational Equity and the Rethinking Schools group based in Milwaukee provide but a few of these examples.[77]

Thus, the original impulse of social reconstructionism to connect schools to progressive social purposes is not dead. It has re-emerged not only at the level of theory, but at the level of practice. And it is here where positive signs—not only negative tendencies—can give us some reason for hope.

Even given these emerging tensions within the conservative restoration and the increase once again of alliances to counter its attempted reconstruction of the politics and ethics of the common good, this does not mean we should be sanguine. It is possible that, because of these tensions and countermovements, the right's economic program will fail. Yet its ultimate success may be in shifting the balance of class forces considerably to the right and in changing the very ways we consider the common good.[78] Privatization, profit, and greed may still substitute for any serious collective commitment.

The forces now arrayed against those of us who wish to return to many of the original democratic impulses of social reconstructionism are powerful. The very process of redefining some of our most basic concepts, such as democracy, equality, and so on, by the right has made it that much more difficult. The conceptual tools most often employed by progressives have been partly appropriated and their meanings changed by retrogressive movements.

We are, in fact, in danger of forgetting both the decades of hard work it took to put even a limited vision of equality on the social and educational agenda and the reality of the oppressive conditions that exist for so many of our fellow Americans. The task of keeping alive in the minds of the people the collective memory of the struggle for equality, for person rights in *all* of the institutions of our society, is one of the most significant tasks educators can perform. In a time of conservative restoration and reconstruction, we cannot afford to ignore this task. This requires renewed attention to important curricular questions: Whose

---

[77] For further discussion of this, see Apple, *Teachers and Texts*; Bastian, Fruchter, Gittell, Greer, and Haskins, *Choosing Equality*; David Livingstone (Ed.), *Critical Pedagogy and Cultural Power* (South Hadley, MA: Bergin & Garvey, 1987). "Substance" in Chicago and "Chalkdust" in New York City are other significant examples of such progressive groups.

[78] Hall, "The Great Moving Right Show," p. 120.

knowledge is taught? Why is it taught in this particular way to this particular group? How do we enable the histories and cultures of the majority of working people, women, and people of color (these groups again are obviously not mutually exclusive) to be taught in responsible and responsive ways in schools? Given the fact that the collective memory that *now* is preserved in our educational institutions is more heavily influenced by dominant groups in society,[79] the continuing efforts to promote more democratic curricula and teaching are more important now than ever.

Echoing some earlier social reconstructionist insights, however, this needs to be done in concert with other more political movements that wish to extend the substance of democracy in all of our institutions. Action in education is made that much more powerful, and more likely to succeed, if it is organically connected to democratic social movements in the larger society.[80] Yet, although action on the curricula and teaching that dominate our schools may not be sufficient, it is clearly necessary. For it should be clear that the movement toward an authoritarian populism will become even more legitimate if only the values embodied in the conservative restoration are made available in our public institutions. The widespread recognition that there were, are, and can be more equal modes of economic, political, and cultural life can only be built by organized efforts to teach and expand this sense of difference. Clearly, there is educational work to be done.

---

[79] See especially Michael W. Apple and Linda Christian-Smith (Eds.), *The Politics of the Textbook* (New York: Routledge, 1991).

[80] I have discussed this in greater detail in Apple, *Education and Power*.

2

THE SOCIAL FRONTIER 1934–1943: RETROSPECT AND PROSPECT

James M. Giarelli
Rutgers University

American society, along with world society, is passing through an age of profound transition. . . . In a word, for the American people the age of individualism in economy is closing and an age of collectivism is opening. Here is the central and dominating reality in the present epoch. . . . In the years and decades immediately ahead the American people will be called upon to under take arduous, hazardous, and crucial tasks of social reconstruction: they will be compelled to make some of the grand choices of history, to determine in which direction they are to move, to make decisions which will deeply affect the life of their country for generations and indeed for centuries—decisions concerning the incidence of economic and political power, the distribution of wealth and income, the relations of classes, races, and nationalities, and the ends for which men and women are to live. . . . They must choose among diverse roads now opening before them. In particular they must choose whether the great tradition of democracy is to pass away with the individualistic economy to which it has been linked historically or is to undergo the transformation necessary for survival in an age of close economic interdependence. In the making of these choices persons and institutions engaged in the performance of educational functions will inevitably play an important role. . . . Whatever course they pursue they will either retard or hasten the adjustment to the new realities, they will either make easy or difficult the transfer of the democratic ideal from individual to social foundations.

Already a few voices have been raised within the ranks of educational workers in acceptance of the challenge of social reconstruction. But as yet these voices are too timid to be effective, too tentative to be convincing, and too individual to speak a language of clear-cut purpose. . . . Before these persons, and perhaps countless others who have thus far remained inarticulate, can hope to become a positive creative force in American society and education, they must come into closer communication, clarify their thought and purposes, draw like-minded individuals into their ranks, and merge isolated discordant voices into a mighty instrument of group consensus, harmonious expression, and collective action. To contribute to the achievement of this object, The Social Frontier is being launched.[1]

"*When intellectuals can do nothing else, they start a magazine.*"[2]

Somewhere between the optimism of the opening quotation and the cynicism of the latter lies the problematic focus for understanding the role of intellectuals in social change and for interpreting the history of modern reform movements. It is through this dialectic, between knowing and doing, clarity and commitment, intelligence and action, that I would like to discuss the radical and progressive educational journal published between 1934 and 1943, *The Social Frontier.*

Born out of the "Kilpatrick" discussion group, and closely associated with the development of the "Social Foundations" of education program at Teachers College, *The Social Frontier* was launched in 1933 as an immediate response to the crisis of the

---

[1] "Orientation," *The Social Frontier*, 1(1), (October, 1934), pp. 3–4.

[2] Irving Howe, (Ed.), *Twenty-Five Years of Dissent: An American Tradition* (New York: Methuen, 1979), p. xv.

Great Depression and its social and cultural implications and as a more generic attempt to embody the broad-based progressive interpretations of the scope and function of educational study.

It would be easy to argue the case for its failure. As C. A. Bowers wrote, the confused and zealous polemical arguments found in the journal "helped to discredit progressive education in the eyes of the public and split the progressive education movement into factions that dissipated its strength in internecine fighting."[3] Agreeing with the fact of its failure, but for very different reasons, Walter Feinberg in *Reason and Rhetoric* argued that though the journal began a promising debate based on "two conflicting analyses of American society,"[4] class-based versus interest group, it was short-lived and quickly succumbed to the consensual progressive ideology of reformism.

There is much to bear out these negative evaluations. At the height of disenchantment with the status quo and of serious considerations of radical alternatives, *The Social Frontier* could barely attract enough readers to maintain operations. Despite attracting a luminous list of contributors, from all the widely read and respected theoreticians of the progressive education movement, to shapers of the international cultural climate, such as Charles Beard, Harold Laski, Norman Thomas, and Leon Trotsky, the journal never attracted a large following among classroom teachers or even among those for whom it claimed to speak in the John Dewey Society, the Progressive Education Association, or progressive teacher organizations or labor unions.

In the early years, there was not much question which broad political road to follow. Dewey once noted that although there once had been much discussion of the intellectuals turning left, "there is no longer such a discussion; the intellectuals are left. . . . The only question is how far left they have gone."[5] The problem was not capitalism versus some form of collectivism, but which form. Adamantly against the New Deal for its reformism, the Social Frontiersmen debated communism, socialism, and even

---

[3] C.A. Bowers, *The Progressive Educator and the Depression Years* (New York: Random House, 1969), pp. 197-198. Also see C. A. Bowers, "The Social Frontier Journal: A Historical Sketch," *History of Education Quarterly*, IV (September, 1964), p. 179.

[4] Walter Feinberg, *Reason and Rhetoric* (New York: Wiley, 1975), p. 211.

[5] John Dewey in A.M. Bingham and Selden Rodman, *Challenge to the New Deal* (New York: Falcon, 1934), p. vi.

fascism. However, by 1936 Roosevelt was supported, albeit reluctantly and conditionally, and by 1942 the journal supported the war, "the American way as a mixed economy," and a new "bill of rights" with a plank on the importance of free enterprise. Although this critique is accurate, it is descriptive of much more than *The Social Frontier* and advances our understanding of the reasons for the ineffectiveness of American radical social thought, historically and currently, very little.

In contrast, some assessments of *The Social Frontier* seem prepared to accept too little. Lawrence Cremin wrote in *The Transformation of the School*:

> To look back on *The Social Frontier* is to contemplate a fascinating episode in the history of American reform. It was without a doubt one of the authentic progressive voices of the thirties; and while its excellence was not consistent, its vitality was.[6]

Raymond Callahan, in *Education and the Cult of Efficiency*, went beyond this in his praise of *The Social Frontier* as "a journal which in its short life was the most outstanding and courageous journal American education produced."[7]

There are good reasons to accept these views also. While the journal *Progressive Education* was publishing articles on teaching methodology and subject matter specializations, *The Social Frontier* was publishing Earl Browder, Leon Trotsky, and Lawrence Dennis; taking on the Hearst Publication conglomerate for its red-baiting journalism; fighting the Rugg textbook censorship case; and arguing for the relevance of Karl Marx, class-based social analysis, and indoctrination for a genuinely democratic education. Yet, although vitality and courage also are descriptively accurate and indispensable for reformers, admitting their existence does not help us to penetrate the fundamental intellectual and practical problems with which the Frontiersmen struggled and with which I believe we continue to struggle.

As Michael Apple wrote:

> We need only recall what stimulated the early social reconstructionists in education to begin to realize that one of the

---

[6] Lawrence Cremin, *The Transformation of the School* (New York: Alfred Knopf, 1961), p. 233.

[7] Raymond Callahan, *Education and the Cult of Efficiency* (Chicago: University of Chicago Press, 1962), p. 203.

guiding themes in past curriculum work has been the role schools fulfill in the reproduction of an unequal society. While these individuals may have been too much optimistic in viewing schools as powerful agencies in redressing this imbalance, and while a number of them ultimately backed away from large scale structural alterations in our polity, the principle of examining the linkages between cultural and economic institutions is a valued part of our past. It is time to make it our present as well.[8]

Transcending the question of success or failure, I discuss *The Social Frontier* in terms of its project. I agree with Patricia Graham's assessment that *The Social Frontier* presented the responsible radical position of those educators who wanted the schools to lead in social rebuilding and that in the vicissitudes of its history we find a microcosm of many problems of the Progressive Education Association and of the progressive education movement as a whole.[9] However, I would like to extend this to argue that these particular efforts to formulate a radical (in the "root" sense) perspective on American educational problems and solutions reflects the problem of modern American radicalism as a whole. The problem has been and can be formulated in many ways. How do we preserve the individualistic values of the older community while simultaneously transmitting them into a new social, collective, or communal democracy? Is it possible to develop a political state powerful enough to deal with corporate wealth, still preventing that state with its augmenting power from being captured by the force we want to control or from becoming repressive itself? These kinds of questions were central to the public conversations of the 1930s and set the tone for *The Social Frontier* debates. As Edmund Wilson wrote in "An Appeal to Progressives" in 1931, "I believe that if the American radicals and progressives who repudiate the Marxian dogma and the strategy of the Communist Party hope to accomplish anything valuable, they must take communism away from the Communists, and take it without ambiguities or reserva-

---

[8] Michael Apple, *Ideology and Curriculum* (Boston: Routledge & Kegan Paul, 1979), p. 42.

[9] Patricia A. Graham, *The Progressive Education Association: From Arcady to Academe* (New York: Teachers College Press, 1967), pp. 70-73, 128-133.

tions."[10] Theodore Brameld, writing in the first issue of the Marxist journal *Science and Society*, made much the same point when he drew a distinction between Marxism as a system of philosophy and metaphysics and Marxism as a social methodology. In this view, the fundamental element of a Marxist analysis, class struggle, is interpreted as a social hypothesis, not as an ontological reality divorced from history and circumstance.[11] As Merle Curti pointed out, it was neo-Marxism that influenced many of *The Social Frontier* thinkers[12] and through their debates and in articles such as Sidney Hook's "What is Living and What is Dead in Marxism?,"[13] they contributed to the development of democratic-humanist Marxist thought, though this contribution has been largely ignored. Thus, whereas it was easy to develop the case for the isomorphism of the two positions and the potential power in their fusion, the intellectual and practical path was fraught with difficulties.

As George Harrison in his full-length study of *The Social Frontier* expressed it:

The Social Frontier offers an example of the tension generated on the one hand by a philosophical tradition which would deny that any particular form of social order exhausts the meaning of democracy and on the other hand by the programmatic thrusts of the Marxian tradition which were far more explicit about the shape of the social order.[13]

It was when this tension was entered most boldly that *The Social Frontier* was at its best and when it can instruct us most as a

---

[10] Edmund Wilson, "An Appeal to Progressives," *New Republic*, LXV(841), (January 14, 1931), pp. 234–238.

[11] Theodore Brameld, "American Education and the Social Struggle," *Science and Society*, I , (Fall, 1936), pp. 1–21. Cited in George J. Harrison, "An Historical Analysis of *The Social Frontier*: A Journal of Educational Criticism and Reconstruction," Unpublished doctoral dissertation, Rutgers University, 1968. Throughout this chapter I have drawn from Harrison's close reading and careful scholarship, although differing from his interpretations in important ways.

[12] Merle Curti, *Social Ideas of American Educators* (Totowa, NJ: Littlefield, Adams & Co., 1968). pp. xxx–xxxiii.

[13] Sidney Hook, "What is Living and What is Dead in Marxism?," *Frontiers of Democracy*, 6(53), (April 15, 1940), pp. 218–220. In 1939, the publication of *The Social Frontier* was assumed by the Progressive Education Association and the title was changed to *Frontiers of Democracy*.

[14] Harrison, "An Historical Analysis of *The Social Frontier*," p. 20.

philosophical and historical resource and as a lens into the fundamental questions for an emancipatory and democratic education. Although they were, of course, unable to solve the problems of, as they wrote in 1936, "uniting the economic realism of the Marxian . . . with the values of the genuine liberal tradition of America,"[14] they recognized that the precise nature of the linkages between cultural and economic institutions forms the basis for any radical educational theory.

In the remainder of this chapter, I trace briefly how this tension was manifested in one of the most important debates in the journal over the question of indoctrination. Finally, I comment on the lingering nature of these tensions and the problems they give rise to in contemporary educational thought.

All genuine education is both constraining and liberating. That is, although education provides us with alternate models of the good life and the critical capacities to reflect and act on their realization, not all choices are presented and not all models of knowing are encouraged. This is simply to recognize that all education, as it acts to conserve and create, springs from a choice of value or a point of reference. There is no such thing as an objective, value-free, or neutral education. But does this mean all education must be some form of indoctrination? Is any attempt to influence, direct, impose, guide, or direct the educated about some point of view about the nature of the good life, even if this point of view is supported by reasons and evidence, an instance of manipulation? Does this present a conflict between the methods we use and the ends we seek? Is the idea of a democratic education inherently biased? What is the relationship between democratic means and democratic ends? These questions, expressible in a variety of forms, were at the core of a long-running conversation in *The Social Frontier* and are a reflection of the tension cited earlier. How do we maintain the respect for freedom of inquiry, individual choice, and tolerance so central to democratic thought while recognizing the powerful forces of nondemocratic educative institutions in shaping and determining individual and social life?

Standard interpretations of *The Social Frontier* debate on these questions make it seem as if the positions taken were clearcut, either–or choices. In this view, one group, believing that neutrality was impossible and that the "crisis" situation and movement of history demanded a vigorous commitment to a

---

[15] "Toward a United Front," *The Social Frontier*, 2(4), (January, 1936), p. 104.

well-defined social vision (democratic socialism), advocated a no-nonsense program of indoctrinating students into the norms and attitudes of democratic collectivist citizenship. In contrast, the opposing group, although holding to the same public vision, believed that democratic ends could not be achieved through nondemocratic means and that the democratic faith required a belief that the natural workings of creative and critical intelligence on the social issues at hand would lead to a commitment to democratic ideals.

In reality, the positions taken were much more complex. Thus, Sidney Hook, in arguing for "The Importance of a Point of View,"[15] wrote that all experiencing begins from a point of view and that the only choices are about what view should be adopted and how it should be used and held. These choices in turn must be based on "the concrete practical context of a particular, time, age and society."[16] For Hook, alternate educational and social points of view must represent a class point of view and "the selection of a social point of view in education means the adoption of a class point of view."[17] Hook then considered the existing class structure and concluded that neither the "owning" class nor "middle" class ideology provides a basis for a liberating education. For Hook, it is only the social point of view of the working class that aims:

> To realize as rapidly as possible a classless society in which the educational process and the social process are different aspects of the same thing. It is not merely as a worker but as an educator that the teacher . . . must adopt the point of view of the working class. For it is only in a classless society that the extension of the fullest educational opportunities to all . . . becomes possible. Creative intelligence, which is the central value of every enlightened philosophy of education, becomes a *social* value and a *social* fact only when the social *conditions* which make impossible the free exercise of creative thinking in every phase of every culture have been removed.[18]

---

[16] Sidney Hook, "The Importance of a Point of View," (Part I) *The Social Frontier*, 1(1), (October, 1934), pp. 19–22 and "The Importance of a Point of View," (Part II) *The Social Frontier*, 1(2), (November, 1934), pp. 17–19.

[17] Hook, "Importance of a Point of View," (Part I), p. 19.

[18] Hook, "Importance of a Point of View," (Part II), p. 17.

[19] Ibid., p. 18 (Emphasis in original).

For Hook, these class conflicts are not resolvable through "methods of experiment and intelligent inquiry because the operation of a class society makes it impossible to entertain basic interests as hypotheses whose validity is to be tested by controlled experiment."[19] Class points of view cannot be compromised "because the essential problem is first to remove the obstacles to intelligent resolution of *all* human conflicts in every field—and the *primary* obstacle to this, although of course not the only one, is the existence of class society itself."[20]

In these quotes Hook seemed to take a clear-cut view. The nature of the linkages between economic and cultural institutions makes a genuine education impossible in a class society. Educators *qua* educators must take their stand with the workers. A democratic society cannot depend on the free interplay of intelligence in educational institutions to resolve differences in some sort of compromise that will serve all interests equally well. There must be a direct and conscious alignment of educators with the ends of the working class and a commitment to using whatever means are necessary to ensure that the interests of this class predominate in educational and social contexts.

But then Hook appeared to waffle. Many conflicts are not "social" and do not spring from a class orientation. For these conflicts, the method of intelligence is our only justifiable alternative. As he wrote:

> The possibility that common interests and ideals will be shared and, where not shared, permitted to flourish side by side in friendly tolerance, is a genuine one . . . the only point of view which allows for its realization is one which takes as its central value . . . *critical intelligence*. . . . This, then, is the only permissible absolute—the only possible attitude which seeks to do justice to the relativity of interests and their objectivity, to both the necessary harmonies in life and the enjoyable diversities of personality, to the presence in every life of security and adventure. The instruments of critical intelligence are not perfect but they are the only one we have which can settle the problems that threaten to

---

[20] Ibid., p. 19.
[21] Ibid., p. 19 (Emphasis in original).

destroy social life and at the same time raise those problems whose consideration is man's greatest glory.[21]

However, if social views and conflicts are expressions of class differences and if these differences are not resolvable through the method of intelligence, then to what kinds of nonsocial value conflicts was Hook referring? How do the "personal, group, clique, and other social oppositions" he mentioned escape being colored by class position? And even admitting that these sorts of class-free conflicts do exist and are amenable to resolution by critical intelligence, how does the practicing educator know the difference between class-determined and class-free conflicts in order to use the correct approach? Finally, and more fundamentally, if the present class system disallows the development of critical intelligence, especially among the working classes (remember Hook argued, "Creative intelligence becomes a social value and a social fact only when the social conditions that make *impossible* the free exercise of creative thinking in *every* phase of culture have been removed")[22], how can we rely on critical intelligence as our only genuine approach to democratic education and democratic society?

Dewey seemed to hold much the same position. On the one hand, he wrote:

> The objective pre-condition of the complete and free use of the method of intelligence is a society in which class interests which recoil from social experimentation are abolished. It is incompatible with every social and political philosophy and activity and with every economic system which accepts the class organization and vested class interest of present society.[23]

Nonetheless, Dewey wanted to rely on the method of intelligence as the means of bringing about the abolition of the class society, which is the objective precondition for the development and use of intelligence in the first place. Seemingly never doubting the correctness of his interpretation, he argued by analogy:

> How do those of us who believe that the advance of science and technology is creating a new pattern of social life, and is

---

[22] Ibid., p. 19 (Emphasis in original).
[23] Dewey cited in Hook, "Importance of a Point of View," (Part I), p. 22.

producing a new type of social conflict between the privileged and the under-privileged, come to that belief? Did we arrive at it by a process of inculcation or by what we regard as an intelligent study of historical and existing forces and conditions? If the latter, and if the method of intelligence has worked in our own case, how can we assume that the method will not work with our students, and that it will not with them generate ardor and practical energy? The realization that the school has and must have some social orientation raises but does not settle the question of the method by which a new social orientation shall be brought about. Till the latter is faced, the whole subject of indoctrination remains ambiguous.[24]

This was to be Dewey's continued argument, that the recognition of the class-based nature of the economic and social systems and the interference of these systems with the development of creative intelligence and democratic life set the problem for democratic educational reformers, but did not clearly define it or the means for its resolution.

Boyd Bode is often thought to represent the anti-indoctrination position. And indeed, as J. J. Chambliss wrote, Bode was adamant in his criticism of his fellow progressives "whenever he found expediency replacing intelligent planning, or indoctrination instead of thinking or the assumption that the answers are in before the appropriate questions are asked."[25] Bode believed that the essential meaning of democracy was to be found in its faith in experimental intelligence and that "to tie this method up with any specific program of reform was to pour out the baby with the bath."[26] The democratic educator must seek "to promote sincere and careful reconstruction in the beliefs and attitudes of pupils, without attempting to predetermine conclusions."[27] Democratic education then refers to methods and procedures, but not to the conclusions reached. But Bode was no simple romantic,

---

[24] John Dewey, "The Crucial Role of Intelligence," *The Social Frontier*, 1(5), (February, 1935), p. 33.

[25] J. J. Chambliss, *Boyd H. Bode's Philosophy of Education* (Columbus: The Ohio State University Press, 1963), p. 33.

[26] Boyd H. Bode,"Democratic Education and Conflicting Cultural Values," *The Social Frontier*, 5, (January, 1939), p. 106. Cited in Harrison, p. 159.

[27] Boyd H. Bode, "Dr. Bode Replies," *The Social Frontier*, 2(2), (November, 1935), p. 43. Cited in Harrison, p. 159.

nor did he believe education could be neutral. The first topic heading in one of his most important articles on indoctrination was "Partisanship is Inescapable." He wrote that "in view of the fact that we are encompassed by this struggle between 'individualism' and 'collectivism' it is futile to insist that the schools must have no part in it."[28] For Bode the question was not one of indoctrination versus education, the first somehow tainted by a "frame of reference," a point of view, or a social commitment; the second being impartial, neutral, objective, and nonpartisan. Rather, the question was one of ends and means. How is the inescapable frame of reference to function in educational practice and does it shape intended outcomes or merely provide a background and context for the free play of intelligence to operate?

As John Childs and the editors of *The Social Frontier* asked, however, is a reconstruction without direction still reconstruction?[29] And if Bode wanted to use a frame of reference for defining the areas and problems to consider, wasn't he inevitably influencing the kinds of conclusions that would be reached? Wouldn't it be more ethically and pedagogically justifiable to admit this and then offer reasons for the worth of the point of view chosen? As the editors wrote, it was fine to hold to the ideal that the respect for the pupils' personality demanded that they be allowed to formulate their own philosophy, but in the present social arrangement "opportunities for thinking, experiencing and experimenting are closed to them." Thus, the purpose of a democratic education was to "fashion a society where respect for personality will have a genuine meaning. As between devotion to the letter or spirit of "respect for personality" *The Social Frontier* chooses the latter alternative."[30]

But what this meant in practice was still confused. In October 1935 the editors urged that teachers should give their pupils a "labor orientation,"[31] but in the following month they argued that teachers should not fix their opinions on students, but

---

[28] Boyd H. Bode, "Education and Social Reconstruction," *The Social Frontier*, 1(4), (January, 1935), p. 18.

[29] John Childs, "Professor Bode on 'Faith in Intelligence,'" *The Social Frontier*, 1(6), (March, 1935), pp. 20–24; "Economics and the Good Life," *The Social Frontier*, 2(3), (December, 1935), pp. 72–73.

[30] "The Position of the Social Frontier," *The Social Frontier*, 1(4), (January, 1935), p. 32.

[31] "Teacher and Labor," *The Social Frontier*, 2(1), (October, 1935), p. 7.

merely select "significant data from the life of society past and present" and trust the students to formulate a "realistic philosophy of social reconstruction." Through the efforts of educators in representing the facts of social reality, the illusions of a classless society can be overcome and "Americans will have made considerable headway toward the goal of democratic collectivism."[32]

Here in this brief summary of some positions taken on the indoctrination debate, I believe we can see the tensions through which *The Social Frontier* material must be interpreted. It was not a question of either–or sides; naïve believers in the powers of intelligence versus hard-headed advocates of specific programmatic actions. Rather the question was about the precise form of the relationship between economic and cultural practices. Ultimately rejecting both the view that the socioeconomic arrangement determines the form of cultural activity and the view that a critical cultural consciousness itself could transform existing social arrangements, *The Social Frontier* sought some dialectical interpretation that would overcome the logic of simple correspondence.

This problem is still at the root of current attempts to formulate theories of radical educational practice. A strong case can be made that the central project of the critical educational scholarship of the last 20 years has been to develop a pedagogy that respects the means–ends continuum and the need to overcome indoctrination through methods of dialogue, demystification, and participation, and also seeks to analyze how the structural and institutional nature of school and social life limit and sanction creative thought. This has often been expressed in terms of the idea of relative autonomy,[33] recognizing the structural and motivational limits on the development of democratic social habits and attitudes within existing cultural and economic institutions, while simultaneously recognizing and encouraging the opportunities for resistance and liberation occasioned by the contradictions inherent within these institutions. In a wonderful essay, Lawrence Goodwyn identified this tension in a

---

[32] "Teachers and the Class Struggle," *The Social Frontier*, 2(2), (November, 1935), p. 40.

[33] A seminal source of this idea is the work of Nicos Poulantzas. See *Classes in Contemporary Capitalism* (London: New Left Books, 1975).

different vernacular and located it at the root of democracy. He wrote:

> A measure of social space exists as a well-earned legacy of hundreds of years of striving in England and America.... Pause for a moment and reflect upon this circumstance, for it represents a fundamental political starting point. The term "social space" is helpful in defining the cultural ... component of non-deferential and generous (i.e., democratic) human behavior. Organizers who are not intimidated and immobilized by the hierarchical nature of their received cultural use available social space to create institutional forms in which democratic ideas—necessarily viewed as insurgent ideas by the larger society—can take life. Such organizers understand that people need to see themselves experimenting in democratic forms. Social space exists to a greater or lesser extent in all societies as a product of the specific political and cultural history of each. Thanks to the organized nature of human striving, there is at least a bare minimum of social space everywhere ... Here, in the primeval drive of the human race for dignity ... is the starting point of democratic theory. And here is the ancestral home of democratic consciousness. The contemporary political challenge is to bring human energy to bear on existing social spaces by creating mass institutions of democracy in them. [34]

I believe that this is the challenge with which the Social Frontiersmen struggled and with which contemporary democratic educational theorists continue to struggle. What are the spaces presented to us for democratic behaviors, those that we have won and those that are a result of the opportunities produced by the contradictions in nondemocratic institutions themselves? How can we widen and deepen these spaces to create mass democratic social arrangements? I suggest that this is not only the problem for democratic educational theorists, as it was for the Social Frontiersmen's educational discussions, but also the problem for American radicalism as a whole. What are the liberating elements of our cultural traditions and how can we use them as a

---

[34] Lawrence Goodwyn, "The Cooperative Commonwealth and Other Abstractions in Search of a Democratic Premise," *Marxist Perspectives*, 3(2), (Summer, 1980), pp. 37–38.

wedge to overcome the repressive element? In doing this, we may borrow from and use historical analyses, interpretations, and strategies, but the model and methods adopted must be homegrown and based on a concrete analysis of the existing state of affairs and its genesis. There are lessons to be learned from work elsewhere, but unless a radical program reflects accurately the conditions in which people find themselves, it will be pure theory with no connection to the tissue of our experience. This is a point increasingly recognized by critical social theorists in a way that supports the continuing relevancy of the tradition represented by the *The Social Frontier*. For example, as the editors of the classically continental critical theory journal *Telos* wrote, "It took communicative action and universal pragmatics to make us appreciate Dewey's pragmatism, Mead's symbolic interactionism, or James' psychology. Thus, the intellectual task is clear. Radical thought in the U.S. has to rediscover its American roots and take it from there."[35] The same point was made recently by Robert Westbrook, author of a critically acclaimed book on Dewey:

> Intellectuals are tired of running into a dead end because of our Marxist jargon. . . . With Dewey we can smuggle our radical views into the conversation without getting stopped by knee-jerk anti-Marxists. We have seen the problems of importing Continental theory, and people are interested in a radical figure in the American grain who has grappled with the issues and democracy and realized that going all the way left or right doesn't work.[36]

The Social Frontier tried to develop just this kind of American radicalism. Some tried to Americanize Marxism, some to radicalize Americanism; almost all struggled with the tensions of bringing distinct but related historical traditions to bear on the analysis of a concrete cultural crisis. The path they eventually chose and its consequences are, of course, very important. But it is also important to remember that it is much the same path we walk on and that our quarrels are within the family. In Volume 5, 1939, the editors wrote, "It may take until 1980, but the march

---

[35] Juan Corradi and Paul Piccone, "Introduction," *Telos*, 66, (Winter, 1985–1986), p. 3.

[36] Robert Westbrook quoted in Robert S. Boynton, "Philosophy in the Woods," *Village Voice* (September 17, 1991), p. 45.

toward ultimate triumph has begun." Well, maybe, but to ensure that it continues we must not ignore or superficially dismiss these first steps taken.

3

"RED TEACHERS CAN'T SAVE US": RADICAL EDUCATORS AND LIBERAL JOURNALISTS IN THE 1930s*

James Wallace
Lewis and Clark College

"Every vibration that agitates the social structure must sooner or later reach the public school." In April, 1929, 6 months before the stock market crash, John Dewey quoted these words of George Counts in the pages of *The New Republic*.[1] Given the economic and political disasters about to befall the world in the next 15 years, this statement was a prescient reminder that the American school is inevitably one of the arenas in which critical issues are fought out. As the major institution that deliberately shapes

---

* "Red Teachers Can't Save Us" was the title under which Agnes de Lima submitted her response to George Counts' articles titled "Education For What?" in *The New Republic*. Her reply was printed in Vol. 71 (August 3, 1932), pp. 317–318. This chapter is a revised version of a paper presented at a joint meeting of the Midwest History of Education Society and The American Educational Studies Association in November, 1987. The author is grateful for the suggestions of Kenneth Benne, now deceased, on an early draft of this chapter. The broader context within which the events of this chapter take place is explored in James M. Wallace, *Liberal Journalism and American Education, 1914–1941* (New Brunswick, NJ: Rutgers University Press, 1991).

the next generation, the school becomes the locus for struggles over those matters about which Americans care most deeply.

In our own time, former Secretary of Education William Bennett continually used the "bully pulpit" of his office to call on the schools to promote traditional social and economic values. A Tennessee judge in a case described as "Scopes II" ordered the removal of textbooks that allegedly supported a secular humanism offensive to fundamentalist families. Business interests constantly call on the schools to adopt curricula designed to meet their specific needs for workers. Minorities and feminists work through courts, legislatures, and school districts to demand belated justice from resistant educational bureaucrats. Thinkers like Stanley Aronowitz and Henry Giroux call for a class-conscious effort by teachers to redress the conservative social balance and to prepare students to take an active part in radical social change.[2]

This contest over the control of schools—and through them the minds and values of the young—has persisted throughout American history, and will doubtless continue to occupy the attention of our pluralistic society. If this struggle should ever cease, we will know that the schools have become marginalized and irrelevant.

An examination—from the standpoint of liberal journalism—of an earlier version of this conflict may serve to remind educators and their allies that it is both persistent and important. This inquiry should provide some perspective on our present situation and remind us that, whatever form current social and political dialogue may take, educators have a fundamental responsibility to help students develop a clear understanding of existing society and the intellectual and moral resources to participate in constructive social change. It may also remind educators of their need for the kind of thoughtful encouragement and criticism that liberal journalists continue to provide.[3]

---

[1] John Dewey, review of George Counts' "School and Society in Chicago," The New Republic, 58, (April 10, 1929), p. 231.

[2] John B. Judis, "Mister Ed: Or, Dr. Bennett at the Bridge," The New Republic, 196, (April 27, 1987), pp. 16–19; Edward Jenkinson, "The Significance of the Decision in Scopes II," Phi Delta Kappan, 68, (February, 1987), pp. 445–450; Stanley Aronowitz and Henry Giroux, Education Under Siege: The Conservative, Liberal and Radical Debate Over Schooling (South Hadley, MA: Bergin & Garvey, 1985).

[3] For some recent examples of such analysis, see "Inside Schools: A Special Report," The New Republic, 205, (December 16, 1991), pp. 7–8, 13–33; Deborah W.

In February 1932, with the American economy continuing its plunge into depression, George Counts challenged the Progressive Education Association's annual meeting with the question "Dare Progressive Education Be Progressive?" He praised the successes of the new education but denounced its middle-class orientation, and called on teachers to indoctrinate their students concerning the failures of capitalism and to prepare them to participate in the building of a socialist society. Later that same month he extended these ideas in two related addresses: "Education Through Indoctrination," to a meeting of school superintendents, and "Freedom, Culture, Social Planning, and Leadership" to the National Council on Education.[4]

With crusading zeal, Counts tried to reach as many people as possible with his radical message. In April, he presented his Progressive Education Association address in the Association's journal under the title "Dare the School Build a New Social Order?" That same month he published the three addresses in a widely distributed John Day pamphlet with the same title. And, wanting to reach noneducators as well as teachers, in May he published the essence of the pamphlet in two articles in the influential liberal journal *The New Republic*.[5]

It was understandable that Counts should choose *The New Republic* to carry his message to a broad liberal audience. From its founding in 1914, that journal, like its older companion weekly *The Nation*, had taken a special interest in educational matters. As David Seideman wrote, the founders of *The New Republic* intended for it to "take the lead in a national renewal in education, literature, and government."[6] During the 1920s—lean years for liberals politically—its editor, Herbert Croly, had emphasized education as part of a long-range program of reform. After Croly's death in 1930, his successors, particularly managing editor Bruce Bliven, continued to give sustained attention to

---

Meier, "The Little Schools That Could," *The Nation*, 253, (September 23, 1991), pp. 321, 338–340.

[4] Counts' addresses marked the beginning of the social reconstructionist movement among progressive educators. The most comprehensive account of this movement is given by C.A. Bowers, *The Progressive Educator and the Depression: The Radical Years* (New York: Random House, 1969).

[5] The pamphlet has been reprinted a number of times, most recently with a new and insightful preface by Wayne Urban: "Dare the School Build a New Social Order?" (Carbondale: Southern Illinois University Press, 1978).

[6] David Seideman, *The New Republic: A Voice of Modern Liberalism* (New York: Praeger, 1986), p. 10.

educational matters.[7] As the depression deepened, both *The Nation* and *The New Republic* described its effects on educational programs and struggled to develop appropriate educational positions with which to confront the crisis.

The liberal journalists and their allies respected Counts and looked to him for helpful insights. John Dewey had favorably reviewed in *The New Republic* Counts' 1928 book on the Chicago schools, which was among the first studies to clearly show the effects of social class bias on education. In 1935 Oswald Villard, *The Nation*'s publisher, wrote to John Dewey to ask his opinion of Counts as a possible editor for that journal.[8] The respect was mutual; as Tyack, Lowe, and Hansot said of Counts and his fellow reconstructionists, "their inspiration was more often the *New Republic* than the *New Masses*."[9]

Counts' first *New Republic* article, published in May 1932, was titled "Education for What?: The Ten Fallacies of the Educators," and was a cogent description and critique of the myths of individualism and impartiality that had rendered schools and teachers irrelevant. The idea that the schools should let children grow without any sense of direction was "the doctrine of laissez-faire, driven from the field of social and political theory, seeking refuge in the domain of pedagogy."[10] His second article, subtitled "Indoctrination and a Workable Democracy," went beyond the critique of fallacies and set forth a challenge to teachers to "seek power and then strive to use that power fully and wisely in the interests of the great masses of people." Teachers would have to accept a new reality: that "our democratic tradition must of necessity evolve and gradually assume an essentially collectivistic pattern." Teachers could no longer be neutral on economic and political issues but had to "assume unprecedented social

---

[7] Interview with Bruce Bliven, Stanford, CA, August 28, 1965.

[8] Dewey's review is cited in Footnote 2. On Villard's interest in Counts as a possible editor, see his letter to John Dewey, September 25, 1935, Villard Papers, Houghton Library, Harvard University. Dewey's reply has not been located.

[9] David Tyack, Robert Lowe, and Elisabeth Hansot, *Public Schools in Hard Times: The Great Depression and Recent Years* (Cambridge, MA: Harvard University Press, 1984), p. 25. See pp. 25–27, 57–69 for a sound interpretation of the reconstructionist movement.

[10] Counts, "Education—For What?: The Ten Fallacies of the Educators," *The New Republic*, 71, (May 18, 1932), pp. 12–16.

responsibilities," accept the new vision of a socialized democracy, and bring it into the schools as "the supreme imposition."[11]

Recognizing that Counts' controversial statements deserved a critique, the editors invited Agnes de Lima, a progressive educational journalist, to reply. She submitted her response with the provocative title "Red Teachers Can't Save Us," but the editors published it under the innocuous label "A Communication."[12] De Lima declared that Counts' call for indoctrination in the schools was no different from numerous other efforts to impose social theories on children. She noted that prohibitionists, utility companies, and fundamentalists all tried to use the schools to propagate their messages, and added that "schools run by Free Thinkers, Single Taxers, Mormons, Seventh Day Adventists, Theosophists, and pink Socialists each reflect the dominant philosophy of those in control." She reminded readers that the Catholic Church, Napoleon, Bismarck, and the Russian Communists all had used the schools to promote their own versions of truth.

De Lima, a feminist and socialist, was sympathetic with Counts' social goals, but was adamantly opposed to indoctrination, and felt that Counts was grossly unrealistic in expecting the teaching profession—"a class long trained to social docility"—to take the lead in social reconstruction. De Lima cited Counts' own 1930 book, *The American Road to Culture*, on the conservative nature of the American school. She quoted her old friend Randolph Bourne in defense of her critique, and turned finally to Rousseau—a hero of child-centered educators—for authoritative support: Counts might disagree with Rousseau, but Rousseau appeared "not merely the better pedagogue, but the more realistic social revolutionist as well." She thus maintained the position she had taken in her widely read 1925 book, *Our Enemy the Child*, that child-centered education was consistent with a long-range program of reform.[13]

C.A. Bowers, in his history of these events, cited de Lima's reply as one of the "most effective and direct criticisms of the

---

[11] Counts, "Education—For What?; Indoctrination and a Workable Democracy," *The New Republic*, 71, (May 25, 1932), pp. 38–41.

[12] Interview with Agnes de Lima, New York City, November 18, 1965.

[13] Agnes de Lima, "A Communication," *The New Republic*, 71, (August 3, 1932), pp. 317–318. *Our Enemy the Child* (1925) was based on articles that had appeared in *The Nation* and *The New Republic*, and was published in *The New Republic*'s series of dollar books.

social reconstructionists" and said that—in questioning the power and wisdom of teachers as leaders in radical social change—it "struck at one of the idealistic, but wholly unexamined assumptions underlying social reconstructionist thinking."[14]

Wayne Urban recently made a similar point in writing that if Counts had

> studied closely the values that permeated much of the teaching force, the ideological predispositions of the very classes from which most teachers were drawn, and the conditions of control under which teachers were working, he would not have been as sanguine about the prospect of teachers leading a social and economic reconstruction.[15]

Other issues of *The New Republic* carried letters in response to Counts' articles, as well as a rebuttal by Counts, but the editors took no stand on the matter.[16] They gave Counts a forum for his position and in the interests of fair play and intellectual dialogue asked de Lima, a leading proponent of the child-centered position, to reply. But they apparently felt that this was a dispute for the educators to settle among themselves and merely provided space in which they could attempt to do so.

In 1933 another forthright statement of educational radicalism appeared in *The Educational Frontier*, a book edited by William Heard Kilpatrick. It included chapters by a number of leading progressive educators, including John Dewey, Boyd Bode, V.T. Thayer, R.B. Raup, H. Gordon Hullfish, and John Childs. Although the authors specifically rejected indoctrination, they did propose that the schools involve students in far-reaching and critical social analysis, believing that such a program would

---

[14] Bowers, *The Progressive Educator*, pp. 38–39; Harold Laski also pointed out the vulnerability of teachers: "A New Education for a New America," *The New Republic*, 87, (July 29, 1936), p. 343. Tyack, Lowe, and Hansot cite Laski's article: *Public Schools*, pp. 61–62, 64.

[15] Wayne Urban, "Teacher Activism," Chapter 7 of Donald Warren (Ed.), *American Teachers: Histories of a Profession at Work* (New York: Macmillan, 1989), p. 197. Gerald Gutek made a similar point, and cited de Lima, in *The Educational Theory of George Counts* (Columbus: Ohio State University Press, 1970), p. 181.

[16] For a discussion of a dialogue between psychologist Augusta Alpert and Counts, see Lawrence Cremin, *The Transformation of the School: Progressivism in American Education, 1876–1957* (New York: Knopf, 1961), p. 250.

produce adults willing and able to participate in fundamental social change.[17]

Sidney Hook, who reviewed the book for *The New Republic*, called it "by far the most progressive and significant statement of the new educational philosophy which is emerging from the depression." He was impressed by the book's profound social analysis, its "radical reformulation" of educational theory, and its politicization of the philosophy of education. But for Hook, who had supported the Communist candidate for president in 1932, the book did not go far enough. It lacked a clear willingness to embrace the class struggle as a necessary instrument of social progress: "Political power has never passed from the hands of one class to another without class struggles; if the classless society is to be achieved, it is not by closing one's eyes to existing class struggles but by prosecuting them more widely and vigorously and intelligently."[18]

This was as radical a statement of political and educational theory as one could expect. But Bruce Bliven and George Soule, the chief editors of *The New Republic*, would not go that far. Although they were sympathetic to what liberals consistently called "the Russian experiment," and though they hoped for a collectivized economy in the United States, they never wholly embraced the doctrine of class struggle as applicable to American conditions.[19] They still believed that nonviolent, rational means might usher in the democratic, socialist society that was their goal. And they were never quite dogmatic enough about their social beliefs to propose that they be imposed on American youth.

The Nation explicitly rejected the idea of indoctrination in the schools. In 1935 the editors reported a speech by Jesse Newlon to school superintendents in which he declared that the teacher should teach as an absolute fact that "capitalism is not the solu-

---

[17] William H. Kilpatrick (Ed.), *The Educational Frontier* (New York: Century, 1933). For rejections of indoctrination, see pp. 71ff. (Dewey and Childs), pp. 146ff. (Kilpatrick), and pp. 211–212 (Thayer).

[18] Sidney Hook, "Education and Politics," *The New Republic*, 75, (May 24, 1933), pp. 49–50. On the positions of Hook and other intellectuals during this period, see Harvey Klehr, *The Heyday of American Communism: The Depression Decade* (New York: Basic Books, 1984), Chapter 4, "The Intellectuals Go Left." For Hook's version of the events of the 1930s, including the role of the liberal journals, see his autobiography, *Out of Step: An Unquiet Life in the 20th Century* (New York: Harper & Row, 1987), Chapters 11–19.

[19] Frank Warren, *Liberals and Communism* (Bloomington: Indiana University Press, 1966), pp. 16–21; Seideman, *The New Republic*, Chapter 9.

tion to the nation's difficulties." The editors sympathized with Newlon's hope that more liberal thinking might penetrate the schools, and were aware that "much academic freedom too often means no more than a tame conformity." But *The Nation* believed that education could not:

> Logically be regarded as a process of indoctrination unless one accepts the doctrine that final truth has been discovered and that learning must henceforth be concerned chiefly with the spread and preservation of that truth. So long as one believes that knowledge grows and changes, one must believe that the younger generation has a right to compare and question, and that free inquiry, not indoctrination, is the ideal of education.

The editors acknowledged that academic freedom was under attack more by conservatives than by radicals, and they hoped for a greater recognition in schools of the leftist position. Like Newlon, they looked forward to a new and better social order, but declared that "nevertheless, the new society will need the critical spirit as much as the old one does, and the conception of free inquiry should not be lost."[20]

The Social Frontier, a radical educational journal founded in 1934 by the Teachers College reconstructionists and edited by George Counts, Norman Woelfel, and Mordecai Grossman, took *The Nation*'s message as an example of "the futility of much current thinking about education." An editorial stated that *The Nation*'s educational philosophy was characterized by a

> vague concept of freedom. . . . Collectivism becomes in this viewpoint only a theoretic alternative to capitalism which should, of course, be discussed—in the abstract—but not to the extent that youth be given the understanding that civilization itself depends upon our taking immediate steps forward to a social order in which inspiring vistas of cul-

---

[20] Editorial, "Propaganda and the Schools," *The Nation*, 140, (March 13, 1935), p. 293. *The Nation* was edited at this time by Freda Kirchwey, Joseph Wood Krutch, and Raymond Gram Swing. Kirchwey was chief editor. Her relationships with progressive education and with the popular front are explored in *Freda Kirchwey: A Woman of "The Nation,"* (Cambridge, MA: Harvard University Press, 1987), Chapters 1-6.

tural accomplishment replace the faded ideals of business enterprise.

Teachers should not shrink from giving social truths to students: "the platitudinous affirmation, 'there is something to be said for both sides' " was therefore outmoded. The piece closed with a mangled metaphor that said more for the writer's passion than for his editorial skill: "Veritably, teachers must sow the seed and society must learn not to fear the whirlwind."[21]

At this point, in 1935, the editors of *The Social Frontier*, with their promotion of indoctrination for collectivism, were more radical on educational matters than either *The Nation* or *The New Republic*. (This was probably the first time that an educational magazine was farther left than the liberal weeklies.) But, although the journals differed on this issue, they agreed with many fellow liberals and radicals that an effective fight against fascism required a popular front with the Communists. The editors of *The Social Frontier*, for example, were opposed to the resignation of non-Communists from the Communist-dominated New York local of the American Federation of Teachers (AFT). An October 1935 editorial declared: "If liberal and labor forces cannot form a united front, if they continue to weaken themselves in bitter factional and sectarian struggles, there is no hope."[22] But Counts, partly in response to the Moscow trials, became increasingly disillusioned with the popular front, and began to part company with the Communists. By 1938 he was leading the fight to break the hold of Communists on the AFT, an effort that finally succeeded in 1939.[23]

Beginning with the issue of October 1937, *The Social Frontier* was edited by George Hartmann, with William H. Kilpatrick as chairman of the editorial board. Hartmann and Kilpatrick opposed the popular front, and were not reluctant to criticize the Communists. In December 1938, the editors wrote that "*The Social Frontier* glories in the fact that real live Stalinists have no use for our brand of democratic collectivism." And in May 1939, they informed their readers of the pressures to which they had been subjected ever since they "began to whack away at

---

[21] Editorial, "A Liberal Weekly Comes Out for Freedom," *The Social Frontier*, 1, (April, 1935), pp. 7–8.

[22] Editorial, "A Plea for Unity," *The Social Frontier*, 2, (October, 1935), pp 3–4.

[23] William Eaton, *The American Federation of Teachers, 1916–1961* (Carbondale: Southern Illinois University Press, 1975), Chapter 5.

Stalinist influence within the Teachers Union, the American League for Peace and Democracy, the American Student Union, and other organizations which the Communist Party considers worthy of its attention."[24]

Under Hartmann and Kilpatrick the promotion of indoctrination also disappeared from editorials. Unlike Counts, Kilpatrick had consistently rejected indoctrination as a legitimate instrument of education. In 1933 he had written in *The Educational Frontier*: "History has convinced the modern-minded that doctrines themselves have their life histories of birth, acceptance, and decay. With this conception of continued change and becoming, propaganda and indoctrination do not fit."[25]

Kenneth Benne pointed out that the Frontier group as a whole never supported indoctrination; rather, for a period of time some of the editors promoted radical proselytizing by teachers as a necessary means of social change. In fact, a continual dialogue on the topic was carried in the pages of *The Social Frontier*, most notably in the January 1935, issue which carried a variety of views by Catholics, Communists, fascists, and liberals.[26]

With the editors of *The Social Frontier* thus moving away from dogmatic radicalism, and *The New Republic* and *The Nation* still maintaining the popular front, by 1938 the journals appeared to have switched sides on some of their earlier positions. Actually, *The New Republic* and *The Nation* had not perceptibly modified their policies; rather, *The Social Frontier* had moved back to a more traditional liberal position. Thus, when another dispute arose, *The Nation* appeared to be to the left of *The Social Frontier*.

James Wechsler of *The Nation*'s staff precipitated the next debate. In 1938 he wrote an article titled "Twilight at Teachers College." He looked back to the heady days of 1934 when the "insurgent voices" of men like Counts, Jesse Newlon, and Harold Rugg were integrating their "educational theories with fresh insights into capitalist disorder." But since that time "internal autocracy and pandering to external conservative interests" had forced the faculty back into line. The college had seen "a pro-

---

[24] *The Social Frontier*, 5, (December, 1938), p. 68; 5, (May, 1939), p. 228.

[25] Kilpatrick, "The New Adult Education," in *The Educational Frontier*, pp. 146–147.

[26] Kenneth Benne, letter to author, January 20, 1989. See also Bowers, *Progressive Educator*, Chapter 3. On p. 108 Bowers noted the "factionalism within the social reconstruction group" after February 1936.

nounced decline in progressive activity, perhaps best exhibited in the doldrums which afflict the *Social Frontier*, and important defections from the teachers' union."[27]

Among these disputatious writers, it is not surprising that Wechsler's vigorous attack elicited an immediate response. (Presumably the editors sent an advance copy of the article to those being criticized.) The next week *The Nation* published a letter from a group of Teachers College professors, including Counts, Childs, and Rugg, which claimed that the article "identified one of the oldest liberal journals in the country with the political sectarianism which has given pattern to the article." They declared that the piece was "full of insinuation and misrepresentation. Taken as a whole it is profoundly false and misleading. We see in it the hand of a political sect in American life which operates on the principle that it will destroy whatever it cannot rule."[28]

The Nation's editors, stung by this attack, came to Wechsler's defense. They said that Wechsler was "in no way identified with any political sect" (he had assured the managing editor that he had left the Young Communist League before joining *The Nation*), and declared that the professors had failed to challenge Wechsler's facts.[29] But this was not the end of the argument. Two months later *The Social Frontier* carried Counts' detailed six-page refutation of Wechsler's article. This rebuttal, titled "Whose Twilight?," ended with a statement that could have been used as a critique of Counts' earlier support for indoctrination: "One lesson contemporary history teaches with unmistakable clarity—ends and means cannot be separated—undemocratic means destroy democratic ends. Such means if long continued and widely practised may bring twilight both to Teachers College and to American democracy."[30]

One need not follow all the tortuous permutations of these disputes to see the major outlines of the shifting relationships

---

[27] Wechsler, "Twilight at Teachers College," *The Nation*, 147, (December 17, 1938), 661–663.

[28] Letter from Counts and others, *The Nation*, 147, (December 24, 1938), p. 703.

[29] *The Nation*, 147, (December 24, 1938), p. 703. On Wechsler's break with the Communists see his autobiography, *The Age of Suspicion* (New York: Random House, 1953), pp. 118–132.

[30] Counts, "Whose Twilight?," *The Social Frontier*, 5, (February, 1939), pp. 135–140. *The Nation* then issued a final rebuttal: v. 148 (February 18, 1929), pp. 193–194.

between the liberal journals and the reconstructionists. At first, in 1932, *The New Republic* gave a hearing to Counts' proposal that teachers adopt indoctrination for a collectivist social order and printed rebuttals and counterrebuttals on the issue. Three years later the editors of *The Social Frontier* defended indoctrination, whereas *The Nation* opposed it. Up to that point the reconstructionists were more educationally radical than were the liberal journals. Then, at the height of the popular front period, the liberal weeklies and *The Social Frontier* took similar positions in favor of a radical curriculum and in support of Communist factions in the Teachers Union and youth "front" organizations. Near the end of the decade, *The Nation* accused the Teachers College reconstructionist group of timidity in the face of administrative conservatism. Finally, after the breakup of the popular front, the liberal journalists and the reconstructionists took similar radical but nondoctrinaire educational and political positions.

On November 8, 1939, 2 months after the infamous Hitler–Stalin Pact, *The New Republic* published its 25th anniversary issue. The fact that William H. Kilpatrick was asked to write the article on education may be taken as a convenient symbol for the reconciliation of the liberal journals and the frontier group. Kilpatrick's article, "The Promise of Education," specifically rejected the educational patterns of "Germany, Italy, and Russia, with their teaching of totalitarian ideas." Kilpatrick insisted that the schools should prepare the young to analyze controversial issues, but that they should avoid the imposition of ideas:

> If, then, we believe in democracy, we shall avoid indoctrination. The rural individualism of the nineteenth century hardly fits into our industrial twentieth century. Democracy too must undergo continual review and perhaps revision. There is no other safe rule. Democracy, to be itself, cannot indoctrinate even itself.[31]

Agnes de Lima was right: Red teachers can't save us—but then, neither can red, white, and blue teachers, or those of any other political coloration. Teachers by themselves—because of the social factors de Lima pointed out—have neither the power nor the wisdom to provide political salvation. But teachers as

---

[31] Kilpatrick, "The Promise of Education," *The New Republic, 101,* (November 8, 1939—Part II), p. 57.

"transformative intellectuals"—as Aronowitz and Giroux want them to function—can develop the strength and intelligence to participate with other groups in creating and supporting policies that in the long run will contribute to saving society from environmental entropy, war, and injustice.[32]

In many ways the challenges facing contemporary teachers are more difficult than those that confronted the reconstructionists. In the 1930s, the impact of the depression was immediately apparent to all, and the growth of fascism, leading to a world war, was an unmistakable threat. Now we are confronted with the even more dangerous challenges of overpopulation, environmental destruction, and nuclear war. But our crises have become chronic. Our young people have grown up with these threats, have learned to live with them, and many—with a media-driven lifestyle of consumerism and shoddy escapist entertainment—avoid thinking about them. Alerting students to the reality and seriousness of these life-threatening crises will require the best thinking and teaching of our "transformative intellectuals."

But contemporary teachers also have a major advantage over those of the 1930s: strong, effective, socially concerned teacher unions that are not afraid to use their power to struggle for better salaries and working conditions and for improved environments in which students can grow and learn. Both the National Education Association and the American Federation of Teachers work vigorously for many newly defined goals of the reconstructionists. Although not demanding a collectivized economy, they do call for greater public investment in education and social services, resist conservative pressures for censorship, and fight vigorously for racial, gender, and social class justice. And even during what Ira Shor called "the conservative restoration" of the current period, teachers struggle alongside minorities, feminists, civil libertarians, and others who share their social goals.[33]

---

[32] Aronowitz and Giroux, *Education Under Siege*, Chapter 2. In 1933 Norman Woelfel called for similar coalition-building, proposing "active participation by educators and teachers in various organizations of the lay public agitating for social reforms." *Molders of the American Mind* (New York: Columbia University Press, 1933), p. 241.

[33] Ira Shor, *Culture Wars: School and Society in the Conservative Restoration, 1969–1984* (Boston: Routledge & Kegan Paul, 1986). On the possibilities for progressive coalition politics, see Martin Carnoy and Henry Levin, *Schooling and Work in the Democratic State* (Stanford, CA: Stanford University Press, 1985), pp. 266–267.

Shor asked the modern version of "Dare the School Build a New Social Order?": "Can the current crises in school and society be solved without economic restructuring? Can school policy and classroom pedagogy have a significant effect on social transformation?"[34] Inspired by the example of thinkers and activists like John Dewey and Paulo Freire, Shor maintained that educators can participate constructively in progressive change. He quoted Freire's hopeful insight that "there is always space for education to act. The question is to find out what are the limits of this space."[35] And Shor encouraged us to extend those limits in the interest of freedom and social change for students and teachers alike.

As we continue to grapple with these issues, the struggles of the radical educators and liberal journalists of the 1930s may be instructive to us in several ways: Their experience reminds us that, even as we form needed coalitions, we must avoid letting our concerns as educators become twisted by the narrow political agendas of other groups. We must not let our eagerness for immediate political success lead us into the prideful assumption that we already have ultimate political wisdom that we may impose on the malleable minds of the young. We must welcome thoughtful, informed criticism from those who share our conviction that creative social progress is possible and that schools and teachers have a constructive role to play in the struggle for reform.

---

[34] Shor, *Culture Wars*, p. 163.
[35] Shor, *Culture Wars*, p. 161.

4

HAROLD RUGG'S SOCIAL RECONSTRUCTIONISM*

Peter F. Carbone, Jr.
Virginia S. Wilson
Duke University

Harold Rugg was a man with a vision. He saw on the horizon a better society—referred to in various writings as "the great society," "the great technology," and "the great new epoch"—emerging out of the harnessing of America's industrial resources, provided that the American people would consent to large-scale social and economic planning.

More than mere social engineering was needed to bring forth this new epoch, however. According to Rugg, a sound (i.e., more humane, tolerant, socially cooperative) society of lasting duration was also contingent on the development of multitudes of cultured, "integrated" personalities, and, because of its "integrity-producing power," he regarded creative expression in the various art forms as an indispensable element in the production of such personalities.

Rugg was interested, then, in raising the quality of American life in general, not simply in removing social injustice. The economic problem was but one element in the total reconstruction of American life that he felt was necessary. These ideas set

---

*Peter Carbone's contributions to this chapter are in large part adapted with permission from two earlier publications: "The Other Side of Harold Rugg," *History of Education Quarterly*, 11, (Fall 1971), pp. 265–278, and *The Social and Educational Thought of Harold Rugg* (Durham, NC: Duke University Press, 1977).

him somewhat apart from his fellow reconstructionists, many of whom, in Rugg's eyes at least, tended to limit themselves to economic questions and did not therefore take a broad enough view of society and the life of the individual therein.

In the first part of this chapter, we examine these two aspects of Rugg's social thought: his notion of redemption through the arts and his proposals for social engineering. The second section provides an overview of Rugg's social studies textbook series and considers the extent to which the textbooks reflected his social thought. The final section is devoted to a critical analysis of Rugg's views and a brief acknowledgment of his contributions to social and educational theory.

PRESCRIPTIONS FOR SOCIAL REFORM

In order to understand fully Rugg's social thought, it is necessary to grasp the extent to which he was influenced by Van Wyck Brooks. In *America's Coming of Age*, Brooks commented on "the idealization of business" in America and observed that the best minds were drawn into commercial activities.[1] It was in this work that he differentiated so memorably between the "high brows" and the "low brows" in American society, the former being concerned mainly with "high ideals," the latter with "catchpenny realities," and neither coming into meaningful contact with the other.[2] Brooks criticized those authors who had abandoned, he felt, their high ideals and succumbed to commercialism in order to please the low brows, but his more severe indictment was reserved for writers who had retained their high ideals at the cost of estrangement from the mainstream of American life.[3] He maintained that we needed writers who could live in both worlds and map out a middle ground of theory and action between them.

Thus *America's Coming of Age* was more than just a critique of American literature. It was also an invitation to writers to point

---

[1] Van Wyck Brooks, *America's Coming of Age* (New York: B.W. Huebsch, 1915), p. 137.

[2] Ibid., pp. 3–8.

[3] Ibid., pp. 37–70.

the way to a general elevation of American culture. Later, in *Letters and Leadership,* a collection of his *Seven Arts* essays, Brooks wrote: "For poets and novelists and critics are the pathfinders of society; to them belongs the vision without which the people perish."[4] He went on to argue that significant social change was highly unlikely "till a race of artists, profound and sincere, have brought us face to face with our own experience and set working in that experience the leaven of the highest culture."[5] This theme, put forth in *America's Coming of Age,* further developed in Brooks' articles for *The Seven Arts,* and repeated in *Letters and Leadership,* became an integral part of Rugg's social philosophy throughout his career. The middle ground between "vaporous idealism and self-interested practicality" that Brooks wanted writers to occupy was not very explicitly marked out, nor was it entirely clear just how the better life was to be lived. Brooks did outline some of its features, however. For one thing, it involved personality development apart from the quest for wealth. "You cannot have personality," he argued, "you cannot have the expression of personality so long as the end of society is money."[6] In addition to the pursuit of life interests or goals other than the purely economic, the good life included a kind of creative self-expression, a release of personality, that would hopefully be channeled into various forms of useful social activity.[7]

These Brooksian notions could serve almost as a prologue to Rugg's social thought, for the same themes—personality development, disdain for the pursuit of wealth, creative self-expression, and increased social cooperation—may be found in all his major works, particularly in *Culture and Education in America* (1931). Echoing Brooks, Rugg found the American "mass mind" regrettably preoccupied with materialistic and acquisitive goals and unreceptive to the development of indigenous creative expression. With exploitation, acquisitiveness, and social conformity in the ascendancy, the creative mind, he thought, has in large part either been rendered inarticulate or diverted into

---

[4] Van Wyck Brooks, *Letters and Leadership* (New York: B. W. Huebsch, 1918), p. 119.

[5] Ibid., p. 127.

[6] Brooks, *America's Coming of Age,* p. 33.

[7] Ibid., p. 32.

technological or business pursuits.[8] Only a few literary giants (Emerson and Whitman prominent among them) were able to transcend the prevailing climate of opinion and emerge as forerunners of a potentially great native literature.[9]

In 1918, while working (under Edward L. Thorndike) for the U.S. Army's Committee on Classification of Personnel, the first group to use aptitude and intelligence tests on a mass scale, Rugg had been introduced (by Arthur Upham Pope) to Brooks' work, along with that of Waldo Frank, Randolph Bourne, and other contributors to *The Seven Arts* magazine. After the war, Rugg, in preparation for his work on the social studies pamphlets that later matured into his textbook series, began to immerse himself in the works of a number of liberal theorists including Charles A. Beard, Thorstein Veblen, John Maynard Keynes, Harold Laski, R.H. Tawney, the Webbs, Graham Wallas, and many others. At first the new ideas encountered in his reading, clashing as they did with attitudes formed during his youth, had an unsettling effect on Rugg. "I had always believed," he recalled, "that the machinery of industrial civilization was essentially admirable and that capitalism was to be accepted on its proved merits and not really to be challenged."[10] For a time he vacillated between these attitudes and the views of the social critics he was reading, but eventually his investigations led him to discard his earlier assumptions. The effect on him was to instill in his mind an ideal of social engineering along collectivist lines, which took its place in his thinking alongside the already germinating idea of redemption through the arts. In connection with the latter, it is worth noting the import of Rugg's appointment at Teachers College, Columbia University in 1920, for it brought him into personal contact with the avant garde in the New York area. His subsequent participation in Frederick Howe's School of Opinion at Nantucket, his association with creative artists such as Alfred Stieglitz, John Marin, Marsden Hartley, and Georgia O'Keefe in Greenwich Village, and his residence in the art community of Woodstock (after 1930) contributed profoundly to Rugg's intellec-

---

[8] Harold Rugg, *Culture and Education in America* (New York: Harcourt Brace & Co., 1931), pp. 4, 92.

[9] Ibid., pp. 145–146.

[10] Harold Rugg, *That Men May Understand: An American in the Long Armistice* (New York: Doubleday, Doran & Company, 1941), p. 202.

tual development, especially to his interest in the nature of the creative process.[11]

Thus in the 1920s Rugg was influenced from two directions. On the one hand, he was plunging into the available library of social criticism and feeling the thrust of various arguments for social engineering; on the other, he was seriously investigating the views of those who felt that artists and writers should lead the way to social uplift. The two strains were to mature in him during the 1930s and provide him with a dual approach to social reconstruction that was rather distinctive among educational reformers. His proposals for collective social action have received due consideration in the educational literature, but the other side of Rugg's reformism, the insistence that we look to the creative artist for guidance in the quest for the good life, has for the most part been neglected in published works.

A Program for Collective Action

Rugg's most specific suggestions for social engineering appeared in *The Great Technology* (1933). The ideas presented in this book were inspired in part by Thorstein Veblen and Howard Scott (leader of the technocracy movement that gained a wide following during the early 1930s), both of whom had proposed that in the interest of efficiency, control of the economy should rest with engineers and technicians rather than with financiers who were interested only in profits.[12] Rugg, a former engineer himself, had long admired Veblen and had made a careful study of Scott's views in the early 1930s. Although his own proposals differed from theirs in specifics, the call was essentially the same: for technological experts to design and operate the economy in the public interest. Hence Rugg took the word *engineering* in the term *social engineering* quite seriously. He wrote:

> The scientific student recognizes at the outset only two factors: a people needing physical goods and a physical world containing the resources from which these can be

---

[11] Ibid., pp. 320–322.

[12] See Thorstein Veblen, *The Engineers and the Price System* (New York: The Viking Press, 1921); Howard Scott, *Introduction to Technocracy* (New York: Technocracy, 1936). Scott had been expounding his theories for years in Greenwich Village before the publication of this book.

produced. The economic problem, then, is to design and operate a system of production and distribution which will produce the maximum amount of goods needed by the people and will distribute it to them in such a way that each person will be given at least the highest minimum standard of living possible. Thus the scientific student does not recognize the right of any person to take an undue share of the goods produced *until all have received that minimum* which the scientific study of physiology and psychology determines is necessary for the maintenance of a healthful life and which the study of the national resources shows is possible. Whether some persons, on account of greater creative ability and initiative, should be permitted to take more than the minimum and how much more is a question that can be answered only by future social experimentation. Personally I should say they should, with definite restriction of the "ceiling" to a low multiple of the minimum.[13]

In passing, we might note Rugg's interesting assertion in this passage that a value question involving the distribution of goods (i.e., who should receive what) is to be answered by experimentation. It is worth noting in this connection that the failure to distinguish between factual statements and value judgments is a recurrent problem in his writings. We return to this point later when we come to our discussion of Rugg's selection of content for his social studies textbooks.

In any case, Rugg believed that the nation possessed an abundance of natural and human resources. The problem, therefore, was to plan and design the economy to take advantage of this abundance. "It is now axiomatic," he said, "that the production and distribution of goods can no longer be left to the vagaries of chance—specifically to the unbridled competitions of self-aggrandizing human nature."[14] In Rugg's view the choice (if it could be called that) was between the economic security that could be achieved through social reconstruction and the social chaos that seemed imminent under a system of laissez-faire capitalism. In order to avoid the latter, Rugg recommended three steps toward

---

[13] Harold Rugg, *The Great Technology: Social Chaos and the Public Mind* (New York: The John Day Company, 1933), p. 106.

[14] Ibid., p. 172.

reconstruction: design, consent, and technical operation under democratic control.[15]

By *design* Rugg meant planning for an economic and political system through the cooperative efforts of technologists, political scientists, philosophers, psychologists, economists, and artists.[16] *Consent* meant a supporting body of public opinion made up of the intelligent minority. He considered himself a "realist" on this point. His experience with mass testing during the war had apparently convinced him that universal understanding of political and economic issues was unlikely in a complex industrial society. He was prepared to settle for a well-informed, articulate minority.[17] Finally, *technical operation* meant turning the system over to technicians who would run basic industries such as farms, factories, and mines so that production would be regulated according to consumer needs.[18] The design and management of the system were to be carried out under the authority of elected political representatives who, acting on the wishes of the people, would leave the working details to the experts.[19] Rugg thought this scheme was an ideal merger of democracy and science. "Such a procedure," he claimed, "bears both the democratic and the scientific sanctions. It is based upon scientific design by experts, the adoption of the design by the true consent of the people, and practical administration by chosen legislators, executives, and judges."[20]

Social Engineering: Rugg's Later Writings

Rugg's social thought was generally consistent over the years. He may have been somewhat harsher in his criticism of existing conditions before and during the depression than he was later on, but his social prescriptions remained essentially the same. Moreover, he never repudiated the views set forth in his earlier writings. On the contrary, he frequently took pains in later books to refer the reader to such early works as *Culture and Education* and *The Great Technology* for a better understanding of

---

[15] Ibid., pp. 186–187.
[16] Ibid., p. 172.
[17] Ibid., pp. 199–201.
[18] Ibid., pp. 186–187.
[19] Ibid., pp. 174–175.
[20] Ibid., p. 172.

his then-current position.[21] By the early 1940s, however, Rugg was more willing than he had been during the depression to acknowledge some promise in New Deal policies.[22]

The 1940s and 1950s likewise found Rugg more receptive to the concept of a mixed economy, partly planned and partly unplanned. In a sense, a mixed economy was always his goal, but during the 1930s he was convinced that a large measure of centralized planning was necessary in order to operate the system successfully. His views on this point were more tentative and more hesitant in his later work.[23] Yet, even in this later period, Rugg very definitely wanted an economy designed to an extent that exceeded any planning programs the nation had previously experienced.[24]

THE RUGG TEXTBOOKS

To a considerable extent, the basic outline of Rugg's social thought was reflected in the social studies textbook series that later drew the wrath of a wide assortment of self-appointed censors. The series evolved out of a set of social science pamphlets that Rugg had written and distributed in the 1920s, and it eventually grew into six volumes for junior high school, published by Ginn and Company between 1929 and the mid-1930s. Five of the books were later revised, and by 1939, eight additional volumes had been produced for the elementary grades. The entire series was published under the general title *Man and His Changing Society*. The textbooks were warmly received at first, but by 1941 they had been labeled "subversive" in some conservative quarters, an action that led to one of the most sensational

---

[21] Harold Rugg, *The Teacher of Teachers: Frontiers of Theory and Practice in Teacher Education* (New York: Harper & Brothers, 1952), pp. 278–279, 281, 292, 295–296, 298.

[22] Harold Rugg, *Now is the Moment* (New York: Duell, Sloan & Pearce, 1943), pp. 140–141.

[23] See, for example, *Teacher of Teachers*, pp. 75–76, 164–166.

[24] Ibid., p. 167. Here Rugg called for planning "on a scale that this nation has never succeeded in attaining in the past."

(and instructive) cases of textbook censorship in American history.[25] The furor over the books caught Rugg somewhat by surprise because, according to him, they were designed simply to provide an accurate description of American society and a balanced account of its strengths and weaknesses. Rugg believed that the social studies should introduce students to the controversial social, economic, and political issues of the day, and that particular belief influenced his selection of content for the social studies curriculum he designed for the Lincoln School at Teachers College and for the pamphlets that later became the textbooks.

Selection of Content

Where did he find the problems and issues covered in the pamphlets? Rugg felt that he had a scientific method for selecting content. His procedure was to examine key writings chosen on the basis of recommendations made by a selected list of scholars representing the various social sciences. These advisers were asked to name the books they would analyze if they were seeking information regarding the important problems of the day. From this and other leads (such as an examination of "scholarly" journals), Rugg and his associates compiled a list of some 300 contemporary problems to be used as the heart of their curriculum.[26]

Now the obvious question at this point is, of course, in what sense, if any, may Rugg's method be regarded as scientific? Joseph Schafer, chairman of the Committee on History and Education for Citizenship, was prepared to deny that it was scientific in any sense. In an open letter to Rugg he wrote:

> You condemn "opinion" as a basis of curriculum making. What is the process you describe above if it is not a setting up

---

[25] See Rugg, *That Men May Understand*, Chapters 2 and 4 for a detailed account of the attacks on the textbooks. See also Peter F. Carbone, Jr., *The Social and Educational Thought of Harold Rugg* (Durham, NC: Duke University Press, 1977), Chapters 1 and 5; Virginia S. Wilson, *Harold Rugg's Social and Educational Philosophy as Reflected in His Textbook Series, "Man and His Changing Society"* (Doctoral dissertation, Duke University, 1975).

[26] J. Montgomery Gambrill, "Experimental Curriculum-Making in the Social Studies," *Historical Outlook*, 14, (December 1923), pp. 391-397. Rugg provided further descriptions of his methods in both *Culture and Education* and *That Men May Understand*.

of "opinion"—either your own or that of others chosen by you—as criteria for determining what is "vitally important," "crucial," etc.? Who are the "outstanding thinkers" and how do you select them for obviously you do select them? . . . if your investigator is a social reactionary he will collect opinions from a given group of 'prominent' men; if he is a liberal he will collect from a group largely or wholly distinct from the first, and if he is a radical he will collect from yet another group . . . .After all it is merely "opinion" camouflaged by the cant of a professed "scientific" investigation.[27]

Schafer was right, of course. A glance at Rugg's list of advisers reveals a conspicuous liberal strain, a strain that carried over into his pamphlets and textbooks and resulted in a very definite stance being adopted in relation to the problems considered.[28] Rugg could, and did, argue that he had sought out recognized authorities. Nonetheless, the list is hardly exhaustive, and, as Schafer pointed out, a curriculum designer with a different point of view would no doubt have drawn on an entirely different group. There has to be a value judgment made somewhere in the selection process. Once this is recognized, Rugg's method seemed an eminently sensible one for achieving his desired objectives, namely to alert students to the fact that all was not well in the social order and to start them thinking critically about possible improvements. However, his questionable attempt to clothe his procedure in quasi-scientific attire raised doubts—despite his frequent protestations to the contrary—about his willingness to expose children to dissenting opinions. What is needed here is a candid admission of the value judgment being employed.[29] Moreover, even if Rugg never set out deliberately to impose his point of view on students, there can be little doubt that the books

---

[27] Joseph Schafer and Harold Rugg, "The Methods and Aims of Committee Procedure: Open Letters from Dr. Schafer and Mr. Rugg." *Historical Outlook*, 12, (October 1921), p. 248.

[28] The list appears in Schafer and Rugg, ibid., p. 251.

[29] In contemporary postmodern times, of course, "emancipation theorists" and other current reformers are far less persuaded of the need, or even the possibility of establishing "objective" grounds for their prescriptions. In Rugg's day, though, before positivism had fallen on hard times, some such grounding was sought by most reformers. George Counts, however, was perhaps an exception to this generalization, and his *Dare the School Build a New Social Order?* may be viewed as a precursor to the more subjective approaches currently in vogue.

clearly echo his own socioeconomic orientation. In *Changing Governments and Changing Cultures*, for example, Rugg stated that "The individual workman was completely at the mercy of the capitalist employer, who dictated hours of labor, wages, and working conditions in the factory. The worker had to take what the employer offered him or starve."[30] Such dependence on the part of the worker made it easy for owners to give him low wages and meager or nonexistent benefits. Elsewhere Rugg commented, "It is no wonder that at the beginning of the Industrial Revolution men struck for higher wages, since the amount of food, clothing, and comforts that people could buy with their low wages was pitifully small."[31] Rugg's support for the workers was obvious. He felt that because workers had lost their independence and were at the "mercy" of factory owners, strikes were both practically and morally justified.

Even worse than the job monotony and low wages were the recurring times of unemployment for the worker. Rugg posed this question: "Can there be 'general welfare' and true 'liberty' in a wealthy country in which a large and increasing army of the people are constantly worried by the danger of unemployment?"[32] In an accompanying workbook, as if to answer the question, Rugg asked the students to "write an essay that supports this point: Every man is entitled to the right to work."[33]

Whether entitled to work or not, the point was that many people were unemployed or, if employed, unsure of the length of their employment, and thus living in a very insecure world. Rugg recognized this insecurity and sought to deal with it: "And the bulk of our people do not have real security of living. Why? There is no more important question before the American people than that. And there is no more important question for American youth to try to answer."[34]

---

[30] Harold Rugg, *Changing Governments and Changing Cultures, Democracy Versus Dictatorship: The World Struggle* (Boston: Ginn & Co., 1937), p. 214.

[31] Harold Rugg, *An Introduction to American Civilization: A Study of Economic Life in the United States* (Boston: Ginn & Co., 1929), p. 389.

[32] Harold Rugg, *An Introduction to Problems of American Culture* (Boston: Ginn & Co., 1931), p. 196.

[33] Harold Rugg and James E. Mendenhall, *Pupil's Workbook of Directed Study to Accompany An Introduction to Problems of American Culture* (Boston: Ginn & Co., 1931), p. 21.

[34] Harold Rugg, *Our Country and Our People: An Introduction to American Civilization* (Boston: Ginn & Co., 1938), pp. 548–549.

If workers were seasonally unemployed or, at best, working for very low wages, then it was obvious that many people under the present industrial system were not enjoying a decent standard of living. In both the elementary and junior high school textbooks, Rugg vividly showed the differences in lifestyles among the American people. In *Man At Work: His Arts and Crafts,* Rugg commented:

> But below it (Figure 92) is a mere shack, a house in which a family could live nothing better than a poor life. Scientists tell us that several million Americans are living in farmhouses which are no safer, no more healthful, and at least as ugly as this one.[35]

Some people had a fine standard of living, but many still did not. In *A History of American Civilization,* one subsection was entitled, "Are all Americans sharing in this rising standard of living?"[36] Obviously Rugg thought not, writing, "But it is doubtful, as we have said, whether half of them are receiving enough to maintain their families according to a minimum comfortable standard of living."[37] It is important to note that in addition to pointing out the problems of the workers at that time, Rugg also seemed to have been sowing seeds of discontent among the young students, many of whom were obviously potential workers.

Rugg wanted students to see the various levels of living and suggested as an activity that students visit homes typical of each of the different classes. By visiting the homes of these people, students would see the vast gap in standards and styles of living. The obvious question Rugg asked the students was, "In the richest country of the world why do millions of poor people continue to live in dark, small, unsanitary tenements?"[38]

Such a state of affairs existed within the United States, Rugg said, because of inequities in income. Rugg frequently discussed the inequitable division of the national income in his textbooks. He claimed that in 1900 "It was generally agreed that . . . *one tenth*

---

[35] Harold Rugg and Louise Krueger, *Man at Work: His Arts and Crafts* (Boston: Ginn & Co., 1937), p. 144.

[36] Harold Rugg, *A History of American Civilization: Economic and Social* (Boston: Ginn & Co., 1930), p. 600.

[37] Ibid., p. 606.

[38] *Workbook Problems of American Culture,* p. 11.

of the American people owned nine tenths of the wealth."[39] Rugg stated that "with such an unequal division of the nation's income it is clear that many of our people could not buy the fine things which were available."[40] Rugg then left little doubt in the students' minds that the majority of people were in an untenable position. They were inadequately paid and housed; yet under the present laissez-faire system there was little they could do because the uncontrolled owners could treat them as they wished.

The poor standard of living of many Americans and the insecurity of these same people meant that somebody was not giving them their fair share of America's abundance. Most Americans since the 19th-century Industrial Revolution had not found their income and their standard of living adequate; yet, for the "few" life was abundantly rich. It was these "few" that Rugg proceeded to attack, for these "few" had, through their misuse of power, placed the mass of workers at their mercy. This power gave them control not only of the basic industries but also the resources of the country, the latter of which were shamefully wasted. In *A History of American Civilization,* Rugg commented, "Hence they were unthinkingly extravagant and there was tremendous waste—in everyday living as well as in the production of coal, iron, oil, the cutting down of the forests, and the use of the soil and its products."[41]

The desire for profits led men to waste resources. To ensure ever increasing profits, new industrialists and money interests consolidated themselves into huge monopolistic enterprises that thwarted competition; as a result corporations were formed. Allied with these big all-powerful corporations stood an equally sinister force, the banks that controlled American economic life. In *The Conquest of America,* Rugg posed the following question, and then, lest someone not understand, answered it himself:

> Do you see how the great banks came to play a very important part in the growing industries of the country? They not only controlled the capital of their own corporations but through their directorships they helped to manage and

---

[39] Harold Rugg, *A History of American Government and Culture: America's March Toward Democracy* (Boston: Ginn & Co., 1931), p. 511.

[40] Harold Rugg, *The Conquest of America: A History of American Civilization* (Boston: Ginn & Co., 1937), p. 513.

[41] *A History of American Civilization,* p. 587.

control the capital of many corporations. Big Business, indeed![42]

It was easy for even the less perceptive students to perceive with Rugg's "expert guidance" that a few men and a few big businesses controlled the economic life of the country.

Rugg seemed clearly to question the integrity of these "few." In the *Pupil's Workbook of Directed Study to Accompany An Introduction to Problems of American Culture*, Rugg put these "few" in highly questionable company:

> Who is the criminal? The man who exceeds the speed limit in his automobile? The man who drinks strong alcoholic beverages? The man who steals $1000 from the bank? The man who murders his enemy? The man who charges too high a price for food, rent, or clothing? The man who advertises his product falsely? The man who forces his laborers to work twelve hours per day at starvation wages?[43]

With no government controls or no government intervention on behalf of the workers under the theory of laissez-faire, these "few" lived at the expense of the "many." Needless to say, these "few" wished to preserve Adam Smith's laissez-faire system at all costs. Rugg stated: "As you can readily understand, this idea was eagerly taken up by the merchants and manufacturers in England and on the continents of Europe and North America. If adopted it would give them a free hand to develop their business."[44]

Rugg, to be sure, gave both the pros and the cons of this laissez-faire system in his textbooks.[45] On the face of things it would seem that Rugg was being eminently fair. Yet this tactic also served his particular purposes. For in presenting an unfamiliar negative in contrast to a familiar positive, he was, as it were, raising jarring questions heretofore not raised in the student's mind. This tactic would hardly be missed by laissez-faire's defenders.

---

[42] *The Conquest of America*, p. 437.
[43] *Workbook Problems of American Culture*, p. 30.
[44] *Changing Governments*, p. 195.
[45] Harold Rugg, *Citizenship and Civic Affairs* (Boston: Ginn & Co., 1940), p. 595.

If the "few" wished to keep the laissez-faire system that they controlled, then they must continue to control that which maintained and supported the economic system, the government itself. Rugg categorically stated that the business community had taken over the government. In *A History of American Government and Culture*, there was a chapter entitled "The Rise of Government by Business." Rugg believed that from the beginning of the new nation, the aristocrats thought that "government should be *of* the people, *for* the people but—by the *best* of the people!"[46] After the Civil War the "best" became identified solely with the new industrial and banking giants, and the control of the government "lay in the hands of the rising manufacturers, businessmen, and bankers of the North."[47] In fact, Rugg claimed the rich and well born had always arranged the government to suit their needs and purposes. For example, the upper classes had received what they wanted from the Constitution. In discussing the founding of our country and the writing of the Constitution, Rugg, following the lead of Charles A. Beard, wrote: "The Fathers of the Constitution feared 'too much democracy.' They were afraid of what the majority of people, who did not possess property, would do to the minority, who did. They were afraid of what they regarded as the ignorance and rashness of the lower classes."[48]

Rugg's emphasis on class interest made it very clear to the students that there had always been a definite class division between the "haves" and the "have nots." The difference between the two groups was that the former had the influence and education to get what they wanted from the society.

In his textbooks Rugg made it clear that because the rich had always controlled the government, they would see to it that their interests were protected. They wanted the government to continue a high protective tariff, but they did not want it to interfere with private business or property by controlling wages, hours, or working conditions.[49] In essence, government was to continue to have a "hands off" policy where business was concerned, unless, of course, these were "helping hands."

---

[46] *Government and Culture*, p. 231.

[47] Harold Rugg, *America's March Toward Democracy: A History of American Government and Culture* (Boston: Ginn & Co., 1937), p. 330.

[48] *Government and Culture*, p. 137.

[49] *America's March*, pp. 331-335, 339.

To ensure that government maintained the laissez-faire posture, heads of great corporations forthrightly stated, according to Rugg, that they gave money to many government officials: "Furthermore, they added, *they sought and paid for the services of leaders in both the political parties*—the Democratic as well as the Republican."[50]

With such goings on in government, it was no wonder that there were some protests against the system. Rugg cited protests that began in the late 1800s against the hold that big business had on the government. Even though some people were questioning the business-dominated society and government, Rugg observed that "many people honestly believed that the prosperity of the country depended upon the prosperity of Big Business."[51]

The fact that so many people believed that the country's, and thus their own, prosperity was dependent on the present business structure meant to Rugg that they had been conditioned to think just this. In *An Introduction to Problems of American Culture*, Rugg devoted two chapters to the study of how public opinion was formed; in the revised *Citizenship and Civic Affairs*, one chapter was allotted to this topic. Rugg felt that organizations and institutions had some role in molding public opinion, but that the printed word was extremely influential in this process. However, the problem was that the newspapers merely presented the views of those who controlled them, that is, the natural adherents of laissez-faire and of business-controlled government.[52] According to Rugg, the newspapers aimed at consensus, not controversy, and a particular consensus at that. That is, laissez-faire was the natural order of things and benefited everyone. As Rugg wrote, "Indeed today the average newspaper-reader receives very little accurate information concerning controversies in industry, agriculture, business, international affairs, and the like."[53]

Rugg went further by questioning the integrity of the newspaper tycoons: "Do newspapers influence public opinion by presenting *proved* facts? Authorities differ on this question."[54] The obvious implication of Rugg's remarks is that newspapers print what serves their purposes, not necessarily the truth. He went on

---

[50] Ibid., p. 336.
[51] Ibid., p. 339; see also pp. 340–357.
[52] See *Problems of American Culture*, p. 441; *Citizenship*, p. 548.
[53] *Citizenship*, p. 544.
[54] Ibid., p. 544.

to cite the newspapers' handling of wars as an example of the dominance of bias over fact.[55]

In his writings for the general adult public, Rugg's answer to the chaos, wastefulness, and inequities of the industrial system had been a socially planned or cooperative society. Rugg believed that with planning America could give the "many," not just the "few," a decent standard of living, obviously implying that laissez-faire did just the opposite. In the textbook *Our Country and Our People*, Rugg stated that, "Careful students of this problem assure us that there are enough riches here in America to give every family in the United States a better standard of living, and this in spite of the fact that the American standard is already among the highest in the world."[56]

Rugg admitted that it had been difficult in the past for people to accept anything other than private ownership in the United States, but he stated that times were changing due to the government planning in World War I and Russia's Five Year Plan. To support his belief that planning was the wave of the future, he included a chapter in *An Introduction to Problems of American Culture* entitled "Looking Ahead: The Age of Planning."

In this "new age" Rugg wanted planning on three levels: individual or local, national, and international. In discussing cooperation on an individual basis in *Our Country and Our People*, Rugg reported a conversation with an Indiana farmer who was a member of a cooperative. The farmer stated, "Maybe some things should be 'just our own' and done alone by ourselves; and other things, like those requiring big machines, done together, or cooperatively, with other people."[57]

On the national level Rugg wanted a planned industrial society so that the misery of the "many" could be ended. In *An Introduction to Problems of American Culture*, Rugg devoted 22 pages to "Scientific Planning in Industry," and in the workbook accompanying the textbook, Rugg posed several questions on the matter. Rugg wanted planned production and fairer distribution of wealth. He stated:

---

[55] See Harold Rugg, *Changing Countries and Changing Peoples: Changing Civilizations in the Modern World* (Boston: Ginn & Co., 1938), p. 350; *Citizenship*, p. 544; Harold Rugg, *Changing Civilizations in the Modern World: A Textbook in World Geography with Historical Backgrounds* (Boston: Ginn & Co., 1930), pp. 356–357.

[56] *Our Country and Our People*, p. 549.

[57] Ibid., p. 7.

We need scientifically planned ways of producing food, shelter, and clothing for the people of America. They must be of two types: first, plans to carry on the industries today so that no one will suffer from unemployment; second, far-reaching plans for the future which will produce food, shelter, and clothing more efficiently and will distribute the national income more equitably.[58]

In Rugg's planned society the workers would have security. Rugg asked, "Why, then, should there be so much unemployment and distress? There are many reasons, but the most important ones can be summed up in one phrase—LACK OF PLANNING."[59] Rugg believed that "The basis of a secure and comfortable living for the American people lies in a *carefully planned economic life*."[60] Though Rugg himself failed to develop specific plans and was often vague on this point of planning, it is clear that planning was to be a government function and laissez-faire was no longer to be the order of the day. In the National Recovery Administration (NRA) and the Agricultural Adjustment Administration (AAA) of the New Deal, Rugg saw the beginnings of a nationally planned industrial and agricultural system. Rugg viewed these as examples of initial government planning.[61] To Rugg, then, the trend seemed clear.

Yet, for Rugg, as we have seen, this planned economy with its freedom from economic worries for the workers was not an end in itself. He wished such a freedom for people so they could have time for creative activities. What Rugg had in mind is what we now refer to as *quality of life* issues. A competitive economy has the potential to drain away creative energies in the struggle for economic gain, but in a planned economy there may be a greater possibility for people to express their creativity. Rugg spoke in the imperative when he wrote, "We must read books and paint and do other creative things."[62] Thus, as Rugg viewed it, creative endeavors were highly important to the good life, a life heretofore the exclusive possession of the "few." Rugg expanded the definition of the arts so as to include not just the "few" but the

---

[58] *Problems of American Culture*, p. 197; see also pp. 196–218; *A History of American Civilization*, pp. 601–610 for a discussion of the inequities in incomes.

[59] *Problems of American Culture*, p. 185.

[60] Ibid., p. 597.

[61] *The Conquest of America*, p. 537.

[62] *His Arts and Crafts*, p. 30.

"many." Coincidentally, as Rugg was writing his textbooks, new art forms, both appealing to and often describing the hopes, fears, aspirations, and follies of the common people, were receiving public acceptance. As Rugg wrote, "A whole new range of arts have been produced—the motion picture, high-grade vaudeville, the operetta, the tuneful musical comedy, the dazzling revue, and jazz."[63] For example, one of Rugg's "lively arts," motion pictures, became the medium for those who could not attend Broadway productions. Just as the definition of the arts was expanding, so did the terms *artist* and *craftsman* become more inclusive. In summarizing the tasks of artists, Rugg stated that "these hold true for you as curtainmakers or as garden-makers or as playwriters or as craftsmen of any kind, just as they have held true for the great builders, painters, sculptors, and other artists of history."[64] Indeed, Rugg felt so strongly about cultivating creative impulses in all people both at work and at play that he devoted an entire elementary textbook to this subject, *Man At Work: His Arts and Crafts*, as well as a number of chapters in his junior high school textbooks.

Rugg not only spoke of a planned economy with its resulting freedom for creative endeavors, but also with genuine foresight showed particular interest in planning for the world's natural resources at the national and international levels. Rugg wrote: "Engineers who have studied the problem have planned a gigantic power system which includes the use of all three of our power resources—coal, oil, and water."[65] However, Rugg went further than national control of basic resources; he wanted international control. Rugg stated:

> Thoughtful students of international relations have long urged that an important step be taken; namely that some central world body be created to control and distribute, in the interests of all the people of the earth, the world's basic minerals, like coal and oil, and other raw products which are sources of international friction.[66]

Rugg's interest in international cooperation included many areas other than basic resources. He also brought up proposals

---

[63] *Government and Culture*, p. 545.
[64] *His Arts and Crafts*, p. 17.
[65] *An Introduction to American Civilization*, p. 150.
[66] *Government and Culture*, p. 580.

for international control of world trade and international cooperation in founding a workable credit system, and he espoused world organizations for peace.[67]

Rugg called for a total end to the old isolationism and the cutthroat competition among nations that had often led to war. One of the changes that the Industrial Revolution had brought, with its trading of raw materials and finished products, was a new interdependence among nations and peoples. This new interdependence meant that nations, sections, communities, and people had to have a spirit of cooperation.[68] If cooperation failed, then war was assured: "All this terrible story of the war has shown you what comes when the friendly relations among countries dependent upon one another are destroyed."[69] Rugg's distaste for war was clear: "Is there no possible way to prevent the actual coming of another world war? Those who are interested in a peaceful solution say there is but one answer: international cooperation and control."[70]

Closely tied to his dream of cooperation and control on all levels was the question of property ownership, for Rugg knew well the historic definition of vested interests. This question of public versus private ownership had a long and bitter history: "But in the meantime there has been much hard thinking, much controversial debate, indeed, much shedding of blood and much human suffering, over the question *How shall property be owned?*"[71] People were still arguing and fighting over the question of property ownership. In *Changing Governments and Changing Cultures*, Rugg stated:

> In the democratic countries, however, minority groups of the Left are doing their best to push their governments toward increasing control of private property. To counteract this pressure the wealthy minority groups of the Right are looking to dictatorship as a means of preserving private capitalism.[72]

---

[67] *Changing Governments*, pp. 701, 713–714.
[68] *Citizenship*, pp. 429–430.
[69] *Changing Civilizations*, p. 383.
[70] *Changing Governments*, p. 698.
[71] Ibid., p. 191; see also pp. 649–650.
[72] Ibid., p. 667.

In suggesting that the wealthy, that is to say the "haves," were not unreceptive to dictatorship, Rugg clearly was attempting to foster empathy among students for the "have nots."

Rugg stated that "many people" thought public ownership of basic utilities was a good idea, but he wanted the students to think the matter through and to decide for themselves, though he offered "guidance" in the matter. He posed the question: *"Under which system of ownership and operation of basic utilities— public or private—will the security and advantage of all the people be better conserved?"*[73] Rugg asked this obviously hoping that they would associate private with the "few" and public with the "many."

World War I provided a good example of government control. Because the distribution of goods by the railroads during World War I was handled efficiently with government control, Rugg suggested that:

> Many people came to the conclusion that as the government had efficiently handled this great utility during the last year of the war it proved that the American people as a whole should own and operate railroads, telegraphs, telephones, power plants, and other basic utilities upon which the lives of the people depended.[74]

Rugg's views on public and private ownership of basic utilities and industries were evident in his textbooks.

Rugg's stand on planning, ownership, and control suggested that his own version of collectivism was at least sympathetic to socialistic solutions to economic problems. In one of the workbooks, Rugg asked students to ascertain the desirable and undesirable features of socialism and capitalism.[75] Once again by presenting this problem, he was opening the students' minds to some unfamiliar positives and negatives. Rugg admitted that the questions raised by the socialists were highly significant:

> *The questions raised by the Socialists and their opponents are of the greatest importance. The whole development of*

---

[73] *Government and Culture*, p. 585.

[74] Ibid., pp. 583–584.

[75] Harold Rugg and James E. Mendenhall, *Pupil's Workbook of Directed Study to Accompany Changing Governments and Changing Cultures* (Boston: Ginn & Co., 1937), pp. 28, 54.

the government in the modern world depends upon how they are answered in the years to come. The young people who are now in our schools will be called upon to answer them.[76]

By asking students to think about the questions raised by the socialists, Rugg was underlining the importance of these questions and inviting exploration of them.

In discussing some of the previous cooperative experiments, Rugg stated, "Within a few years New Lanark became famous all over Europe as a model industrial community. Owen's experiment seized the minds of thinking people everywhere."[77] Though they failed in their immediate aims, they left a legacy for our times:

> But Robert Owen and his socialized communities had builded better than they knew. Though they failed ultimately, they had provided the Western world with concrete materials for thinking about the public ownership of property. They had achieved beginnings in the practical working out of cooperative ownership.[78]

Rugg's sympathies for the "thinking people" and the socialist planners could not be lost on even the average reader. In discussing various cooperative experiments, Rugg even gave glowing marks to Russia's first Five Year Plan: "Remember, then, that the first Five-Year Plan included the improvement of every phase of the life of the people—family and community life as well as industry and agriculture."[79] Thus quite obviously Rugg appreciated governmental planning in other nations.

Rugg's Political Persuasion

Rugg's textbooks clearly critique unbridled laissez-faire capitalism and call for a somewhat vague planned society. This critique and call coupled with his stinging attack on the social and cultural effects of capitalism in *The Great Technology* (1933) led some of his critics to the erroneous conclusion that Rugg was, if

---

[76] *Government and Culture*, p. 411.
[77] *Changing Governments*, p. 208.
[78] Ibid., p. 210.
[79] Ibid., p. 445.

not an outright Communist, at least a "fellow traveler." Rugg's critics believed he was so enamored with the Soviet system that he would applaud transplanting the system to American soil. In reply to these charges, Rugg attempted to set the record straight in 1941:

> I am not a Communist. I have never been a Communist. I have never been a member of or affiliated with the Communist party, directly or indirectly, in any way whatsoever. I am not a Socialist. I have never been a Socialist. I have never been a member of or affiliated with the Socialist party. Nor have I taken part in the work of that party.[80]

Rugg was convinced that Marxist theory was largely irrelevant to the social and economic realities of American life:

> Thus, neither from the study of the process of government, nor the history of the American mind, nor from the current eye-witness appraisals, can I find support for the Marxian dictum that the American people are divided today into two antagonistic conflict groups in which a class of propertyless workers will shortly fight it out with a small but powerful propertied class. Moreover, a careful study of the American Marxians' data, which purport to apply Marx's theses to twentieth-century America leaves grave doubts as to their validity.[81]

His rejection of Marxism was based on his conviction that class conflict was inappropriate to describe the American situation. Rugg viewed political reality in the United States as the interplay of many small special interest groups. Hence America, in his view, encompassed a number of "shifting groups, some of which, from time to time, are mutually exclusive and antagonistic, but most of which overlap in membership and intent and are both partly conflicting and partly co-operative."[82] For Rugg, the notion of two independent social classes locked in bitter conflict was simply unrealistic in the American context.

---

[80] *That Men May Understand*, p. 89.

[81] Harold Rugg, "The American Mind and the Class Problem," *Social Frontier*, 2, (February 1936), p. 140.

[82] Ibid., p. 139.

Rugg's attitude toward socialism was less clear. Despite his repudiation of the label, his textbooks, as we have seen, frequently reflected a socialist orientation, and during the depression his books for adults often sounded a socialistic note in criticizing New Deal policies. He objected, for example, to what he felt were tinkering, halfway measures intended to revive private capitalism rather than to accomplish the "fundamental" reconstruction he deemed necessary.[83] In addition, he often made proposals to "integrate" key industries into a national system, to redistribute the wealth, to establish fair-profit figures, to set ceilings on salaries, and to provide for minimum standards of living that were certainly more extreme than the prescriptions of most New Dealers. Thus Rugg's views were perhaps not as far removed from those of the socialist persuasion as his statements to the contrary would seem to indicate.

His exact position is not easy to determine, even with his attempts at clarification. He said, for example, "I believe in private enterprise. But I believe in social enterprise too. I believe we should leave the play of individual initiative as free as possible and in as many areas of life as human ingenuity can contrive."[84] But surely this expression of Rugg's beliefs would be acceptable to representatives of almost any political-economic ideology. The statement can have little meaning until we know how much free enterprise, how much social enterprise, how much individual initiative, and in what spheres of social life. Unfortunately, Rugg did not provide answers to these questions on that particular occasion. In a later book (*Now is the Moment*, 1943), however, he did give us some indication of what he considered to be a desirable balance between free enterprise and social enterprise. Looking back over the depression years from the vantage point of 1943, it seemed to Rugg that such a balance had already been achieved by the Tennessee Valley Authority (TVA):

> And it did come about in that Valley—a fine fusion of centralization of sovereignty and financing, design and total administration, hand in hand with a decentralized owner-

---

[83] For a sampling, see *Great Technology*, p. 105; "Strains and Problems of a Depressed Society," Chapter 4 in *Democracy and the Curriculum*, Third Yearbook of the John Dewey Society, Harold Rugg (Ed.), (New York: D. Appleton-Century Co., 1939), p. 106; *American Life and the School Curriculum: Next Steps Toward Schools of Living* (Boston: Ginn & Co., 1936), pp. 451–452.

[84] *That Men May Understand*, p. xiv.

ship and a "grass roots" operation. Both federal and local authorities, they said, should take part—the federal government doing the things for which it was best equipped, the state and local government doing others, and the private companies, the cooperative associations and individuals doing still others.[85]

Elsewhere he described the TVA as a model of cooperation between public and private interest: "Here we see a Mixed Economy, part centralized, part decentralized—working democratically. Here is the object lesson for a century to come."[86]

It seems fair to conclude, then, that in the 1940s Rugg accepted the TVA as a model for social reconstruction and would have been pleased to see it duplicated wherever conditions warranted. Whether he would also have found it acceptable in 1932 when he was writing *The Great Technology* is, of course, conjecture. He was less disposed at that time to concur with New Deal policies than he was during the 1940s and 1950s. All we can say for sure is that by the 1940s, the TVA represented for Rugg the desirable mixture of public and private enterprise that he had been groping for earlier in his career. There are those who would argue that his wish to extend the type of planning that went into the TVA to other sectors of the economy demonstrated his socialist leanings, but it is also clear that Rugg would reject this appraisal of his position. The point is a disputable one and leaves unanswered the question of exactly where Rugg stood ideologically. The best we can do is plot his position somewhere between New Deal liberalism and democratic socialism and resist the temptation to force him into either camp.

CRITICAL ANALYSIS

Earlier in our discussion we alluded to some difficulties in Rugg's procedures for selecting content for the social studies curriculum (and his pamphlets). Here we extend our critical appraisal of

---

[85] *Now Is the Moment*, p. 32.

[86] Harold Rugg, *Foundations for American Education* (New York: World Book Co., 1947), p. 416.

Rugg's work to his social engineering and his assumption that we must seek moral guidance from creative artists and writers.

Social Engineering

Rugg's recommendations for social planning and action suffer from a scarcity of detail that makes evaluation difficult. Presumably he did not provide an operational description of how his designed system would function because he felt that this task should be undertaken by the designers and technicians themselves. This is fair enough, perhaps, except for his skirting of a fundamental issue that he should have considered, even on the general level at which he chose to carry on the discussion.

The issue involves the relationship between political representatives and those who were to design the economy, a relationship Rugg never clarified. The key question is where does control reside? Now assuming, as Rugg did, that the design and operation of the economic system are to be carried on within a framework of democratic political institutions, control must rest ultimately with the elected representatives of the people, and Rugg said as much himself.

In view of some of the other things he said (and did not say), however, it seems permissible to wonder whether he wished to minimize this control, at least in 1933. It is possible that his reticence concerning the limits of the planners' authority and the mechanism for exerting governmental control over them may have stemmed from a reluctance to explicitly place the experts under the direct authority of political office holders. His problem was to provide the means by which an aristocracy of talent could set economic policy within a democratic framework of government, but he had little confidence, it seems, in the integrity of politicians. He was afraid that under the sway of private business interest and out of self-seeking political motives, they would fail to give the system designed by scholars and operated by technological experts a fair trial. Thus on the few occasions when he discussed their role in the designed system, he did so with an unmistakable note of disparagement. In one passage, for instance, he expressed serious misgivings about the likelihood of freeing politicians from the influence of businessmen.[87] In another, he argued that "the basic industries must be taken from

---

[87] *Great Technology*, p. 180.

the sphere of political manipulation and carried on purely as a scientific and technological enterprise."[88] In still another, he called for "the exertion of public compulsion upon elected officials to put the new design to experimental trial."[89]

All of this conveys the distinct impression that Rugg regarded political representatives and appointees as a necessary evil whose participation in the reconstruction of society should be kept to a minimum. Their role seems to have been reduced to that of performing necessary administrative, legislative, and judicial duties in compliance with the recommendations of expert social engineers who would emerge as the real policymakers. In particular, his statements regarding the administrative function of politicians and the need for public compulsion to ensure their cooperation indicate that he may have desired rather sweeping de facto power for his proposed planning group.

This interpretation of Rugg's position is reinforced by a consideration of his views on popular consent. He insisted that "the consent of an organized body of the people is the desideratum of prolonged stability in social action . . . . The consent of the people is indeed basic to the democratic method."[90] And yet the elitist implications in his outlook are unmistakable for, as we noted earlier, the consent Rugg had in mind was that of an "intelligent minority." In this connection he wrote, "No permanent reconstruction can be brought about that does not rest upon the consent of at least an effective minority of considerable size."[91] He went on to describe the "effective minority" as individuals with sufficient intelligence to understand the complexities of modern society, choose capable leaders, and evaluate suggested policies intelligently. The "rank and file," on the other hand, were described as "followers," many of whom could not be expected to comprehend the difficult problems and issues of contemporary society or the relative merits of proposals for social reconstruction.[92] It was primarily the "thinking minority" that Rugg hoped to enlighten with his program of adult education,[93] and although he did not spell it out in so many words, the tacit assumption was

---

[88] Ibid., p. 175.
[89] Ibid., p. 172.
[90] Ibid., p. 187.
[91] Ibid., p. 187.
[92] Ibid., p. 200.
[93] Ibid., p. 201.

clearly that members of the intellectual elite would help to mold public opinion in favor of social change.[94]

Thus the reconstructed society would be one in which artists and writers provided clues to the "good life," while scholars and technologists designed social institutions, and an intelligent minority built consensus among the people. There is an autocratic ring to this scheme that is faintly audible in much of Rugg's work and that signals difficulties for his concept of democracy as government according to popular consent. In a review of *The Great Technology*, Lawrence Dennis commented:

> For Professor Rugg the problems of the hour are those of design for the new order and consent of the people. Technological experts will draw up the best hypothetical designs for an economic and political system that their cooperative thought can produce . . . . The intelligent minority will then take care of the problem of consent by creating a large supporting body of public opinion . . . . The results will be democratic control and technical operation. To call such an achievement "democratic control" seems to me either a piece of crass stupidity or intellectual dishonesty.[95]

On the whole, Dennis' criticism, particularly his objecting to Rugg's use of the term *democratic control,* was justified but also somewhat harsh. Clearly Rugg was neither stupid nor intellectually dishonest. He was intellectually untidy, however, in that he took an eclectic approach to issues that frequently led him to entertain conflicting ideas. Good democrat (in the broad sense) that he was, Rugg felt that popular consent based on an understanding of the issues was a necessary prerequisite to social reconstruction. At the same time, he felt that only a minority of the population was capable of fully understanding present social conditions, their antecedents, and the need for change. This minority had to be used, therefore, to create a nationwide climate of opinion favorable to social reconstruction. The fact that for

---

[94] He came close to spelling it out in the following passage: "Just as a Tammany precinct leader knows that he carries his precinct if he delivers his allotted 'five votes,' so we can create intelligent social reconstruction if we can produce five thoughtful Americans in each of our million neighborhoods." Ibid., p. 202.

[95] Lawrence Dennis, "Is Capitalism Doomed?" *Saturday Review of Literature,* 9, (May 27, 1933), p. 615.

most people this plan would result in their granting consent based on something akin to conditioning rather than on understanding seemed to have escaped Rugg's notice.

Redemption Through the Arts

Rugg's faith in the ability of creative writers and artists to show the way to the good life (in the moral as well as the nonmoral sense apparently) was based on the highly questionable assumption that there is something almost inherently moral about the creative process. For Rugg the "cultivated" life of the artist is marked by honesty, integrity, a sound personal philosophy of life, and honorable social relationships—a far cry from Rugg's conception of the predominant mode of America, which he described throughout his writings as exploitive, hypocritical, and sadly lacking in integrity. It would appear, then, that he considered the cultivated or cultured life to be "good" in the moral as well as in the nonmoral sense of the term.

But why should this be the case? Why did Rugg think that people who engage either actively or vicariously in creative activities, especially in the arts, are more likely than others to demonstrate integrity? The answer rests in his assumption that if one wishes to successfully complete a creative project, one must be prepared to engage in a good deal of hard work, sacrifice, and self-criticism. It is these activities, Rugg held, that develop self-discipline and moral fiber.[96] Elsewhere he said:

> It is the art experience, the creative act, that contains within itself the psychological power to develop the sound individual and hence the sound society. That power is the concept and attitude of Man-as-Artist's integrity as set forth in the constant attempt to objectify himself—to speak, to write, to make, to do only what he is—I can only conclude, then, that the creative art experience, because of its integrity-producing power, is an indispensable vehicle for social integration.[97]

---

[96] Harold Rugg and Ann Shumaker, *The Child-Centered School: An Appraisal of the New Education* (Yonkers-on-Hudson, NY: World Book Co., 1928), pp. 282–286.

[97] *American Life*, p. 440.

Touching on the same point in another context, Rugg stated: "Between the Man-As-Artist's opinions and his life there will be no gaps . . . . There will be no lacuna between his theory and his behavior. Defense mechanisms will be reduced to a minimum. Hypocrisy will not exist in human behavior."[98]

Rugg reached for altogether too much in these passages. He was probably right in his contention that the self-discipline that is so important a part of the creative process is also a prime factor in the development of character; furthermore, self-expression would seem to be one way of coming to a better understanding of one's abilities, capacities, and uniqueness of personality. The resulting increase in self-awareness, in turn, might be a significant step toward achieving an autonomous individuality that relies mainly on internal norms of conduct rather than on external patterns of conformity. Further, all of this no doubt contributes to one's mental and emotional well-being. Hence Rugg's references to a mental and emotional synthesis, an integrated personality, a "gathering-together-of-the self" are presumably meaningful to the creative artist (and perhaps to the psychologist as well). But even supposing, for the sake of argument, that this is the case, there is still a gap here between the psychological connotations of *integration* and the moral connotations of *integrity* that he bridged too easily in his discussion of the self-expressive, creative person. Given that self-expression is a factor in developing an integrated personality and that the term integrated personality implies mental and emotional stability, one can question the claim that an individual so endowed is also a person of integrity. The term *integrity* connotes moral soundness or uprightness, and these terms suggest the concept of *virtue*. One wonders, then, whether Rugg was implying that the creative or appreciative individual is by definition also a virtuous individual. If this was his intent, he was clearly mistaken, for there is nothing illogical in the assertion that a creative person may be morally deficient. A swindler, for example, or better still a forger, could conceivably be an artist in his or her own right.

Thus it simply does not follow that the creative person is necessarily a person of integrity. It may be the case that creative self-expression is one element in building character or developing integrity, but it seems clear that Rugg exaggerated its importance and offered an approach to individual and social better-

---

[98] *Culture and Education*, p. 232.

ment that is both overoptimistic and rather limited in scope. Unless he can establish a firm connection between creativity and integrity his theory is somewhat unconvincing, and it has been the burden of this analysis to show that the purported connection is problematic at best.

Epilogue

The difficulties alluded to in this discussion inevitably diminish to some extent the thrust of Rugg's proposals for reform, but those difficulties should not be permitted to obscure his accomplishments. It has often been claimed, and with considerable justification, that Rugg's work touched more significant areas of progressive education than that of nearly anyone connected with the movement. Early in his career, for example, he was involved in the pioneering attempts to apply the quantitative methods of science to educational problems. (His *Statistical Methods Applied to Education*, 1917, became a standard in the field.) Then in the 1920s he was identified with the popular child-centered approach to teaching. Indeed Lawrence Cremin called *The Child-Centered School*, which Rugg co-authored with Ann Shumaker, "the characteristic progressivist work of the twenties."[99] During the 1930s he became a leading spokesman for the reconstructionist point of view, and in 1947 he published *Foundations for American Education*, one of the most comprehensive treatments of educational foundations of that (or any) period. Finally, the 1950s found him among the ranks of those searching for the secrets of the creative process.[100]

Rugg also was by all accounts a gifted innovator in the area of curriculum development. In fact, his broad-fields approach to building courses around the fundamental concepts and themes of several disciplines was apparently the first of its kind.[101] He was also a keen critic of traditional educational practices; indeed, his suggestions for change were among the most imaginative put forth by his generation of educators. Further, his social studies

---

[99] Lawrence A. Cremin, *The Transformation of the School: Progressivism in American Education, 1876–1957* (New York: Alfred A. Knopf, 1961), p. 183.

[100] See Harold Rugg, *Imagination* (New York: Harper & Row, 1963).

[101] B. Othanel Smith, William O. Stanley, and J. Harlan Shores, *Fundamentals of Curriculum Development* (Yonkers-on-Hudson, NY: World Book Co., 1950), p. 406.

textbook series was one of the outstanding educational efforts of the 1920s and 1930s; had he never accomplished anything else, this achievement by itself would have sufficed to ensure his niche in the history of progressive education. Rugg was, moreover, a talented synthesizer of current developments in a variety of disciplines. Several of his books, notably *Foundations for American Education* (1947) and *Imagination* (1963), are vast storehouses of information as well as valuable secondary sources for researchers interested in topics on the social and behavioral sciences and problems in the field of education. Finally, his suggestions for establishing closer ties between school and community, for viewing the school as only one among several educative agencies in the community, and for regarding education as a lifelong process taking place in a school-centered community anticipated a number of the innovative educational proposals of the past 30 years. All of this versatility made him one of the most interesting of the reconstructionists and, without question, one of the dominant educational theorists of the progressive era.

5

FEMALE FOUNDERS AND THE PROGRESSIVE PARADOX*

Susan F. Semel
Hofstra University

The beginning of the 20th century in America, referred to as the Progressive Era, was marked by a proliferation of educational experiments inspired by the *new education*, a term synonymous with progressive education.[1] More often than not, these educational experiments took the form of independent, child-centered schools, founded by female practitioners who rejected traditional modes of instruction. Instead, they created educational settings that emphasized the development of the child over the demands of subject matter, cooperation and group life over competition and individual achievement, and democratic practices as preparation for living in a democratic society. These female founders shared some basic values with the Social Reconstructionists such as George S. Counts who challenged edu-

---

* Sections of this chapter are adapted from Susan F. Semel, *The Dalton School: The Transformation of a Progressive School* (New York: Peter Lang, 1992).

[1] For a more detailed discussion of these progressive experiments, see Lawrence Cremin, *The Transformation of the School* (New York: Random House, 1961); John Dewey and Evelyn Dewey, *Schools of Tomorrow* (New York: E.P. Dutton & Co., 1915); numerous case studies exist as well. See for example, Susan Lloyd, *The Putney School* (New Haven: Yale University Press, 1987); Lucy Sprague Mitchell, *Two Lives*, (New York: Simon & Schuster, 1953); Caroline Pratt, *I Learn From Children* (New York: Harper & Row, 1948).

cators to construct a new society through the schools.[2] They were, in many cases, directly influenced by the contemporary example of John and Alice Chapman Dewey's Laboratory School, founded in Chicago in 1896 as a place in which educators might seek "to discover in administration, selection of subject matter, methods of learning, teaching and discipline, how a school could become a cooperative community while developing in individuals their own capacities and satisfying their own needs."[3] Furthermore, these female founders had at their disposal a body of literature John Dewey produced for Laboratory School parents, in particular, *The School and Society* (1899), in which he attempted to explain how the school could act, in the words of Horace Mann, as "a lever of social reform" by addressing the needs of each child and educating for membership within a democratic society. As Dewey eloquently stated regarding the purpose of schooling:

> When the school introduces and trains each child of society into membership within such a little community, saturating him with the spirit of service, and providing him with the instruments of effective self-direction we shall have the deepest and best guarantee of a larger society which is worthy, lovely, and harmonious.[4]

Dewey's words and deeds found fertile ground among a significant group of female practitioners who founded their own child-centered schools loosely based on Dewey's ideas, some frankly more derivative than others. Yet, for all of their preoccupations with the needs and interests of individual children, each in her own particular way created a community within the school in which students would be exposed to the spirit of cooperation and group life. A particular phenomenon that arose in the area of female leadership of child-centered, independent schools, I label the *progressive paradox*. Although female founders regularly espoused the notions of cooperation and group life, they nevertheless, in their personal leadership styles, ruled by fiat, generally quashing democratic impulses from faculty and parents

---

[2] George S. Counts, *Dare the Schools Build a New Social Order?* (New York: John Day, 1932).

[3] Katherine Camp Mayhew and Anna Camp Edwards, *The Dewey School* (New York: Harper & Row, 1936), pp. xv–xvi.

[4] Martin S. Dworkin (Ed.), *Dewey on Education* (New York: Teachers College Press, 1959), p. 49.

with autocratic actions. Recent theories of women in leadership positions fail to explain the actions of these founders; rather, they point to the danger of attempting to impose present models on past practices.

The relationship between the particular form of progressive education advocated by these female practitioners and social reconstructionism is a complex one. On the one hand, their child-centered schools tended to emphasize the individual development of the child and were often more concerned with individual growth than social change. On the other hand, given their emphasis on the Deweyan concept of democratic community, these schools attempted to connect individual growth to group life and had an implicit emphasis on the betterment of society through the schools. Although it is clear that they were not social reconstructionist in the strict sense, as they did not have an explicit agenda for social transformation, these child-centered progressive schools had a limited social reconstructionist agenda: to help create a more democratic society. Finally, given the fact that the student population of these schools was overwhelmingly drawn from the professional and intellectual upper middle classes and the upper class, it is problematic to argue that these schools could be labeled social reconstructionist. Nonetheless, child-centered progressive schools played an important role in the history of progressive education and attempted to balance the dual goals of Deweyan progressivism—individual growth and democratic community—with all of their difficult complexities and contradictions.

Three women and their schools represent very different community configurations. Caroline Pratt's school, City and Country, founded in 1914 in New York City, focused on early childhood and elementary education. Helen Parkhurst's Dalton School was founded in 1919, also in New York City, and accommodated both elementary and secondary school students. Carmelita Hinton founded the Putney School, a progressive, secondary, boarding school in Putney, Vermont in 1934. Although the Putney School was founded considerably later than the other two schools, it nevertheless, represented a fine paradigm of a self-sufficient school community imbued with progressive principles found in Dewey's early writings on educational philosophy. Moreover, unlike the other two schools, which were day schools, Putney as a boarding school enjoyed the luxury of rural isolation, which may have allowed its founder even more freedom to implement her particular vision of progressive education.[5]

CAROLINE PRATT AND THE CITY AND COUNTRY SCHOOL

Caroline Pratt, a former practitioner from Fayetteville, New York, began her school, which would eventually become City and Country, in a three-room apartment in Greenwich Village in the fall of 1914. Influenced by current pedagogical thinking, she attempted "to try to fit the school to the child, rather than as we were doing with indifferent success—fitting the child to the school."[6] However, as will become apparent, Pratt also created alongside her child-centered pedagogy an embryonic community within the school that attempted to mirror a democratic society.

Interestingly, Pratt began her school as a "play school"—a prekindergarten school—based on the notion that children learn by play and that for children, play was really hard work.[7] In particular, Pratt emphasized the use of wooden blocks to help children "sort out and make sense of the world around them."[8] Pratt explicitly stated that the program for the younger children and for the older children as well, was formulated through:

> work with blocks and kindred materials. Play with these materials is an organizing experience. At three or four, children come to block-building, for example, after a good deal of experiencing with their bodies. They themselves have been everything . . . cows, animals of all kinds, engines . . . everything that moves. . . . Now they become interested in the details. What part of the engine makes the whistle? What makes the movement? Who pulls the throttle? Children are interested in these not as mere facts, but as facts to

---

[5] For a more complete discussion of boarding school culture see Peter W. Cookson, Jr. and Caroline Hodges Persell, *Preparing for Power* (New York: Basic Books, 1985).

[6] Caroline Pratt, *I Learn From Children* (New York: Simon & Schuster, 1948), p. 8.

[7] Ibid., p. 9.

[8] Jean W. Murray, "Philosophy and Practice at City and Country," City and Country, unpublished materials prepared for student teachers, c. 1950.

be used in play; or it would be more correct to say that what the information does to the play is to keep it going and help it to organize as a whole, to raise new inquiries and above all to offer new opportunities relationships . . . this is what block-building means to us.[9]

Play, however, for Pratt, was not static; rather, she believed that the play experience leads to new opportunities for further experiences and therefore growth.

Although Pratt began her school with six children from working-class families whose tuitions were funded by outside benefactors, she had difficulty attracting and retaining working-class families from the neighborhood. As she expanded both her preschool and elementary school programs, in a new building that she rented on West 13th Street, she observed:

> We did not get as many children as we had hoped. It was one thing for parents to send their children to *play* school before they were six, but quite another to keep them out of public school and send them to us. They were afraid the children would not be ready for public school later, and they were not far wrong. We had no intention of pushing three R's on the children until we felt they were ready.[10]

However, if working-class families were unwilling to participate in Caroline Pratt's pedagogical experiment, artists and writers in the neighborhood were not. Rather, this group was more willing to embrace unconventional methods and thus the composition of the student body changed dramatically during the school's initial years to include mostly Greenwich Village bohemians, along with some upper class WASPS and German Jews.[11]

Although Pratt began City and Country with a focus on the early years of the child, she began to add more classes concerned with academic content, until the school eventually accommodated children through age 13. The pedagogic practice was frankly Deweyan in nature, based on the needs and interests of children at various ages and heavily slanted toward inquiry and experimentation, book learning, and experience. Pratt believed

---

[9] Caroline Pratt, "Making Environment Meaningful," *Progressive Education*, 4, (April–May–June 1927), p. 105.
[10] Caroline Pratt, *I Learn From Children*, pp. 48–49.
[11] See Ibid., Chapter 4, for a fuller discussion of this phenomenon.

that young children should initially learn experimentally and experientially from their immediate environments; then, as they mature and as their horizons expand, they should be introduced to more sophisticated tasks and materials:

> As the children grow older, they carry their inherent experimental method into other fields with the help of a teacher and a loosely but positively organized program. Jobs require trips to stores to purchase things. A school store requires extended buying at wholesale and selling again at retail. Wholesalers need warehouses for supplies and the children visit there. Finally they begin to require books as sources of information; and through these, with the teacher's help, they extend their inquiries beyond the confines of their own city. They make maps instead of floor schemes. They are pushing back their own horizons.[12]

As the curriculum of the school began to evolve, so did the practice of assigning specific jobs of actual service to the different age groups, so that the school eventually functioned as a self-sufficient community. For example, the Eights (8-year-olds) ran the school store; the Nines, the post office. The Tens produced all of the hand-printed materials for the Sevens, such as flash cards and reading charts, and the Elevens ran the print shop and attended to all of the school's printed needs: attendance lists, library cards, stationery, and so on. The Twelves first made toys, then weaving. They finally settled on the publication of a monthly called *The Bookworm's Digest*, which reviewed new children's books sent to the group by publishers, and included "Old Favorites," a particularly popular column in the journal.[13] As students performed jobs they also learned basic academic skills and more sophisticated principles of economics, for example. What emerged from this model was a community of independent young children who were actively engaged in their learning, while concurrently contributing to the life of their school community.[14] In sum, these students were, to return to

---

[12] Caroline Pratt, "Learning by Experience," *Child Study*, 11(3), (1933), p. 70.

[13] Caroline Pratt, *I Learn From Children*, p. 101.

[14] Although I tend to believe that many of their child-centered schools did create important communities, historian Lawrence A. Cremin takes a less sanguine view in *The Transformation of the School*, cited earlier. Readers would do

Dewey, "saturated with the spirit of service," while learning to be self-directed in the context of the school community—"the best guarantee of a larger society which is worthy, lovely and harmonious."[15]

Although there is disagreement on the actual matter of school governance, it is safe to say that almost from the beginning, Pratt had a semblance of a democratic structure in the form of an executive committee, whose charge it was to oversee business and curricular matters. This committee, elected by the principal and staff, consisted of five to seven members, some parents and some faculty (there was a great deal of overlapping here). Sources generally agree that discussions were open and that Pratt took what was said under advisement. Pratt had a way of making each participant feel as if he or she was making a valid contribution.

Most sources, however, support the notion that although Pratt allowed for the structure of democratic governance, she nevertheless had very clear ideas about her particular version of progressive pedagogy and how it was to be implemented. One graduate, in particular, likened the way the school was run to "national socialism in Russia." She further stated that, "When it came down to brass tacks, she [Pratt] made the decisions. She ran it like Stalin." Furthermore, this source noted that although the executive committee was composed of parents and teachers who were "heavy duty guys who were very affluent," Pratt "would and did dominate these people."

This informant pointed to the fact that the kind of women who served on the executive committee (not unlike a board of trustees) were upper class or upper middle-class women "who liked to come in and drink martinis." Executive committee meetings, in fact, took place in Pratt's office, where participants were greeted by a uniformed maid, who served them cocktails and hor d'oeuvres—the latter usually catered by Luchows Restaurant. Pratt's talent for management lay in the way she "let the women drink martinis while convincing them that she had listened to and taken up their ideas."

As with many of these women founders, Pratt had little tolerance for those who deviated from her philosophy. Thus, some people who taught at City and Country, in another informant's opinion, felt that "the quicker I get out of here the better." Politi-

---

well to consider both points of view; therefore, for a different perspective of Caroline Pratt's school, see pp. 201–207.

[15] Martin S. Dworkin (Ed.), p. 49.

cal differences also discouraged some faculty from continuing at City and Country—especially those who were "to the Left of Caroline." There are reports from former parents and former students of Pratt's highhandedness in her daily dealings with her constituency. Pratt noted these shortcomings herself, although not in detail, in *I Learn From Children*. Perhaps in Pratt's case, as with many other talented leaders who were part of the pedagogical avant garde, the Rousseauean notion of using force to be free was the most viable and expedient solution to nurturing and developing their particular experiments.

Although Pratt's leadership was less than democratic, her creation of an educational community in which students contributed cooperatively toward its maintenance while also learning experientially and through traditional means exemplified Dewey's idea of a school as a "democratic workshop."[16] Pratt believed that "a school's greatest value must be to turn out human beings who could think effectively and work constructively, who could in time make a better world than this for living in."[17] Clearly she attempted to do just that at City and Country. Her school remains today at West 13th Street in Greenwich Village, a small progressive school, struggling to remain true to the vision of its founder while meeting the needs of its students at a dramatically different point in time. But clearly, the vision of its founder is at odds with the way in which she chose to implement it.

HELEN PARKHURST AND THE DALTON SCHOOL

Helen Parkhurst, a practitioner from Durand, Wisconsin, founded The Dalton School in New York City in 1919.[18] Influenced by Maria Montessori, John Dewey, and Carleton Washburne,[19] she created the Dalton Plan, which attempted to

---

[16] Robert Westbrook, "The Dewey School and Workplace Democracy," *Pathways*, 8(3), (May, 1992), p. 7.

[17] Caroline Pratt, *I Learn From Children*, p. 15.

[18] Originally called The Children's University School.

[19] Throughout her career, Helen Parkhurst maintained that her teachers were John Dewey and Maria Montessori. Significantly, she omitted the work of Carleton Washburne, the architect of the individual system not unlike The

provide students with a better way to learn; a plan that would permit them to organize and pursue their studies individually, within an environment that would be conducive to maximum cooperation and interaction between the members of the school community. In essence, Parkhurst, like Pratt, attempted to balance individualism and group life within the school, understanding that her students must ultimately be prepared to live in a democratic society.

In founding The Dalton School, Parkhurst was aided and encouraged by her benefactress, Mrs. W. Murray Crane of Crane Paper in Dalton, Massachusetts. Intrigued by what she had read about Parkhurst, Crane invited her to Dalton in about 1916 to start a school in her home for her young daughter, Louise, and three of her friends. Encouraged by Crane, Parkhurst managed to introduce The Dalton Plan in the local public high school, where it enjoyed a very brief life. In 1919, Parkhurst opened The Dalton School, funded by Crane, on West 72nd Street in New York City. In 1929 the school moved to its present location on 89th Street between Park and Lexington Avenues.

Parkhurst's early educational efforts attracted a great deal of attention. Her book, *Education on The Dalton Plan*, was published in 1922, and within months of its publication, was translated into 14 languages. Essentially, Parkhurst was concerned with creating:

> A community environment to supply experiences to free the native impulses and interests of each individual of the group. Any impediments in the way of native impulses prevent the release of pupil energy. It is not the creation of pupil energy but it is release and use that is the problem of education.[20]

The guiding principles of the Dalton Plan were freedom and cooperation. By freedom, Parkhurst intended the student to work free from "interruption . . . upon any subject in which he/she is absorbed, because when interested he/she is mentally keener,

---

Dalton Plan of Parkhurst. She probably was far more aware of Washburne's work than she was willing to acknowledge. Her work, far from being original, represents a synthesis of the ideas of all three individuals. For a more detailed discussion see Susan F. Semel, *The Dalton School: The Transformation of a School* (New York: Peter Lang, 1992), Chapters 1 and 2.

[20] Helen Parkhurst as quoted in Evelyn Dewey, *The Dalton Laboratory Plan* (New York: E.P. Dutton & Co., 1922), p. 136.

more alert, and more capable of mastering any difficulty that may arise in the course of study."[21] To this end she abolished bells, for she was thoroughly cognizant of the fact that students learn at their own rate and she wished to create a learning environment conducive to their needs. As she dramatically suggested in her book, "Freedom is taking one's time. To take someone else's time is slavery."[22]

By cooperation, Parkhurst's second principle, she meant like Dewey, "the interaction of group life."[23] Concerned with preparing students to live in a democracy, she attempted to create a school in which maximum cooperation and interaction would occur between students and students, students and teachers. To this end she implemented her principle through the work problem:

> Under the Dalton Laboratory Plan we place the work problem squarely before him (the student), indicating the standard which has to be attained. After that he is allowed to tackle it as he thinks fit in his own way and at his own speed. Responsibility for the result will develop not only his latent intellectual powers, but also his judgment and character.[24]

Students, at the beginning of the academic year, would be apprised of the year's work in each subject. They would be required to discuss their plan of action with each teacher, because Parkhurst believed it was essential that both students and faculty members understand their tasks. Later, the students might discuss their action with other students and on their recommendations, modify their chosen course of study; they might even abandon it and start another. This process, although time consuming, nevertheless allowed students to participate in planning their studies with both faculty and students, interacting with the community in the spirit of cooperation.

In addition to planning, cooperation could be achieved through student activities, such as clubs or committees, and the *house system*, an important component of the Dalton Plan. House, particularly in the high school, was conceived of by

---

[21] Ibid., p. 16.
[22] Ibid., p. 16.
[23] Ibid., p. 16.
[24] Ibid., p. 18.

Parkhurst as an arrangement of the student population into small, mixed-aged clusters meeting with teacher–advisors four times per week for a total period of 90 minutes. The content of the house meeting was varied. It might consist of students planning and executing their work; planning an assembly for the entire school community as a group, thus discharging their responsibility to the school community; or it might deal with such mundane annoyances as students' difficulties scheduling appointments with faculty members. House discussions might include personal concerns of individual students as well, because Parkhurst believed that students' attitudes, habits, and experiences had a definite bearing on community life within the school. In sum, house would serve as the institution that would both foster the spirit of cooperation among students and simultaneously encourage the development of the qualities of independence and social awareness among its constituents.[25]

Other components of The Dalton Plan consisted of the contract system, the assignment, and lab. The curriculum was divided into *jobs,* usually encompassing 20-day time periods. Each student would contract for their job and would sign a contract to that effect.[26] Students' tasks appeared on the *assignment:* "an outline of the contract-job with all its parts."[27] *Lab,* conceived of as a means of assisting the student to grow in independence and responsibility, consisted of large blocks of time in the daily schedule (usually each morning from 9 to noon) that were set aside for students and teachers to work together to fulfill contract obligations. Lab could be either a group or individual experience; students could meet with teachers or not; however, each teacher had a lab room and each student was expected to utilize the resources of his or her teachers.

Above all, flexibility was the key to the success of Parkhurst's particular vision of progressive education. Conferences (classes) were called only as needed; classes (grade meetings) too, were called on a need basis and were usually convened to discuss problems common to a particular age group. Parkhurst's Dalton

---

[25] Helen Parkhurst, *Report of the Dalton School to the Commission on the Relation of School and College* (New York: Dalton School Archives, 1937), p. 5.

[26] The younger children, usually in The Middle School, signed contracts. Students in the high school were monitored through progress charts, which required obtaining faculty signatures as their tasks were completed.

[27] Helen Parkhurst, *Education on The Dalton Plan* (New York: E.P. Dutton & Co., 1922), p. 50.

exuded a quality of informality, enormous energy, situational decision making, and a high level of engagement on the part of both its faculty and students.

From its inception, the tone of The Dalton School was set through Helen Parkhurst's personality. She was a forceful, creative, and charismatic individual. Like Caroline Pratt, she engendered great devotion—indeed fierce loyalty—on the part of her faculty, students, and parent body. Her style of leadership, at odds with her pedagogy, was authoritarian, paternalistic, and often nonrational. Nonetheless, these traits were tolerated, and often indulged, by the school community because she was perceived as being both a great educator and a formidable individual. Thus, Parkhurst was able to decide and implement her educational philosophy, expand the physical plant, and oversee financial matters largely unfettered by decisions made by important constituent bodies of the school, such as its board of trustees. As one former board member and admirer remarked of Parkhurst, "You might decide something at a board meeting, but she wouldn't do it."

From the outset, Parkhurst managed to attract a loyal parent body to Dalton through her speaking engagements, publications, and personal contacts. She was also known to read the newspapers, often in search of famous families who might be coaxed into sending their offspring to Dalton if given generous scholarship aid. In particular, she attracted an interesting student body whose parents were mainly engaged in the arts, professionals interested in education, a contingent of German Jews, and some upper class WASPS whose children did not fit in traditional schools—a student body not unlike that of City and Country School.

It is interesting that Parkhurst's management style mirrors that of Pratt. Charlotte Durham, her successor, characterized her as "a benevolent, creative, autocrat," who "cared passionately about freedom for children."[28] Parkhurst was enmeshed in every aspect of the school. She visited the homes of her students; held student, teacher, and parent conferences; and randomly invited students into her office to chat about school or personal concerns. Durham, in fact, continually underscored the point that when Parkhurst was headmistress "she was central and

---

[28] Susan F. Semel, *The Dalton School: The Transformation of a Progressive School* (New York: Peter Lang, 1992), p. 40.

final in its management—very few ideas came from the faculty."[29]

Like Pratt with her executive committee, Parkhurst managed her board of trustees in such a way that she did virtually as she pleased, particularly in regard to educational policies and finances. Informants report that those who forcibly opposed her were pressured until they resigned either for "reasons of health" or "business responsibilities."[30] From 1919 through 1936, Parkhurst ran the school virtually without accountability. Then, in 1936 the board finally began to take action to curtail her power over educational policy "and to accept responsibility of maintaining budget limits established by the Board."[31]

Nevertheless, it was not until 1942 that Helen Parkhurst was forced to resign and the school went into receivership. Several incidents of thoughtlessness and dictatorial management preceded this disaster. The first, a merger with the elite Todhunter School, was accomplished without board or faculty support—or knowledge—until Parkhurst was forced to publicize her actions. The merger proved to be disastrous; few students from Todhunter came to Dalton and questionable financial plans were issued from both sides. The second incident, known as the New Milford Experiment, was a scheme to provide both city and country experience to students, yet no one knows how it came about or how it was financed, save the fact that the locale was chosen because it was site of Parkhurst's recently purchased country house in New Milford, Connecticut. Although the experiment never caught on, the faculty was nevertheless disgruntled by the authoritarian way in which it was introduced. Parkhurst could not account for the sum of $40,000 over the budget, according to board minutes. The third incident, her expansion program in the 89th Street building, was implemented without giving the board notice, and served to underscore her sentiment that the school was hers to direct as she saw fit.[32]

Parkhurst's Achilles heel was money, and in the end she was forced to resign as the school faced bankruptcy. She raised money successfully, but she spent it imprudently. She had difficulty taking direction from faculty and board members, because she believed that the school was her creation, her property; so

---

[29] Ibid., p. 40.
[30] Ibid., p. 40.
[31] Ibid., p. 40.
[32] Ibid., p. 40.

much so that she was incapable of distinguishing between what belonged to her and what belonged to the institution. Her vision of democracy, as she interpreted Dewey, lay in pedagogic practice rather than in school governance.

Today, Parkhurst's school is a large, thriving institution with three sites and a student body more than three times as large as in Parkhurst's era. It has accommodated itself to the educational marketplace and is less progressive, more traditional, and more concerned with achievement and college placement. Its last three heads have been men.

Helen Parkhurst, like Caroline Pratt, was an autocratic leader with a democratic vision. She and Pratt were contemporaries as well as progressive pioneers who established sanctuaries for democratic education, rife with the progressive paradox. The third example, Carmelita Hinton, although founding her school almost 20 years after Pratt and Parkhurst, exemplifies the same paradox.

CARMELITA HINTON AND THE PUTNEY SCHOOL

Carmelita Hinton founded The Putney School in Putney, Vermont in 1935. Hinton's school was remarkable in several ways: first, because it was committed to coeducation for secondary school students during a period when boarding schools for adolescents were predominantly single sex; second, because it was a school with an ideology firmly grounded in the early progressive education movement, although its late founding date (1935) would suggest social reconstructionism; third, because The Putney School represented a genuine attempt on the part of its founder, in Dewey's words, "to make each one of our schools an embryonic community life, active with types of occupations that reflect the life of the larger society, and permeated throughout with the spirit of art, history and science."[33] The Putney School, in particular, provides an excellent example of a child-centered, progressive school that attempted to function as a microcosm of a democratic society, with varying degrees of success.

---

[33] Martin S. Dworkin (ed.), *Dewey on Education* (New York: Teachers Col-lege Press, 1959), p. 49.

What makes Putney somewhat different from many child-centered progressive schools is that it attempted to create a curriculum for students that would be rigorous and college preparatory, while designing a way of life for its students that would allow them to participate wholeheartedly in the life of the community. It is highly probable that no other boarding school charged tuition of $1,400 per child, which guaranteed the students exposure to Latin, German, or French, and also allowed them to experience shoveling manure, feeding pigs, and waiting tables. The Putney School was both a school and a working farm, thus students at Putney had both academic and work commitments and most assuredly, participated in the notion of learning by experience. Finally, Putney School's founder, Carmelita Hinton, exemplified the progressive paradox at work: As an educational innovator she acted most autocratically to ensure the acceptance and continuance of her particular progressive experiment; an experiment that balanced (albeit precariously) child-centered pedagogy with democratic group living.

Carmelita Hinton was born in Omaha, Nebraska. Bryn Mawr educated, she found her way to Hull House in Chicago in 1913, where she remained for over 2 years, first as a part-time secretary, then as a volunteer. Although the Deweys had left Chicago for New York by the time Hinton arrived at Hull House, Addams presided over a community that had more than a passing interest in the "new" education. Thus, it is possible to surmise that Hinton was exposed to such ideas as the Gary Plan and the Winnetka experiment, contemporary progressive experiments in schools in Gary, Indiana and Winnetka, Illinois. Certainly, through her Hull House years, she became exposed to a network of progressive educators, both in public and private sectors, who would offer her continued encouragement and support for her own work.

Hinton remained in the Midwest until 1925. Then, recently widowed with three young children, she moved to Cambridge, Massachusetts, and became a second-grade teacher at the Shady Hill School, an independent, child-centered progressive school. She remained there until 1934, when she took a leave of absence to design her own school, one that would accommodate children seeking a secondary school that was both progressive and residential.

Hinton opened The Putney School in 1935, during the depression. On the surface, its curriculum was traditional because the school was positioned as a college preparatory school. Nevertheless, the teachers at Putney were allowed a great amount of freedom in their individual classrooms to teach to their own strengths and interests. They also had to be extremely flexible and able to individualize instruction because Hinton was committed to a modified Dalton Plan. In reality, this meant that students could learn at their own pace and that they could engage in long-term projects. This method proved most fortuitous for the school, because the student body from the start contained a wide range of ability and age levels. Additionally, its student body tended to be composed of students who had formerly attended independent, child-centered, progressive day schools.

From the beginning it was clear that Hinton set the expectations (especially behavioral) for the students along with the faculty. However, shortly after the school was founded, a community council was established, consisting of seven students and six teachers and staff members, chaired by a student. Students were, in fact, very much aware that their ideas counted. Wrote one, "Our decisions made a difference in school rules and even curriculum."[34]

Although Hinton's school was committed to rigorous academic work, she probably would have pointed to the learning that took place after the academic day ended as equally significant for the students. What made Putney special was that each student had a job that contributed to the life of the community—in this case, a working farm. Thus, students cared for the animals, planted and harvested crops, and worked to maintain the premises as part of the Putney experience, at the same time, helping to ensure the financial success of the farm. Putney students, like City and Country students, not only learned (especially their computation skills) through work but contributed to the life of the community firsthand.

Historian of education Lawrence A. Cremin quoted Colonel Francis Parker's observation that the ideal school should be a "model home, complete community and embryonic democracy."[35] Hinton truly attempted to create a community that mirrored the composition of society and that was democratic through two strategies—the first involving admissions, the second, faculty.

---

[34] Susan M. Lloyd, *The Putney School* (New Haven: Yale University Press, 1987), p. 48.

[35] Lawrence A. Cremin, *The Transformation of the School* (New York: Random House, 1961), p. 132.

During the first year of the school's existence, Hinton granted scholarship aid to 50% of the student body. Although this policy would guarantee diversity, it nevertheless proved impossible to maintain, especially for a school that had no endowment. Thus, the percentage of scholarship aid was gradually adjusted so that Putney ultimately granted aid to 15% of the student body.

In terms of faculty, it is interesting to note that from the beginning students called faculty by their first names, thus lessening age and status distinctions. It is also important to note that little social distinction was made between the academic faculty and "staff" (farm) faculty; that although Hinton paid the staff faculty less, this was a carefully guarded secret, and there was a concerted effort to include the staff faculty in the life of the school. For example, staff faculty members were invited to faculty meetings and almost all of the school committees formed included both academic and nonacademic faculty.

Students and faculty both reported that Hinton was indeed, very serious in attending to the opinions of Putney students. However, she was less so in dealing with her faculty. Turnover at Putney was high, so that a teacher's stay at Putney averaged about 2 1/2 years. Paradoxically, although Hinton was genuinely interested in community decision making, "she ruled like a benevolent despot."[36] As John Holden, a Putney teacher and administrator pointed out, Hinton "wanted things to be completely democratic; "at the same time, "she also wanted them to go the way she wanted them to."[37] Thus, it is not surprising, given the autocratic nature of Hinton and the liberal climate of the faculty, that in 1948 the faculty at Putney went on strike. Although times had changed since the founding of Putney, Hinton continued to proceed as she had in the past, without attempting to address serious issues such as grossly inadequate faculty salaries and housing, hiring, and staffing procedures. Many faculty members were particularly disturbed by the private arrangements Hinton made with her perceived "favorites" regarding housing and salaries; others were concerned with the inordinate amount of power she wielded over their lives, because the rapid turnover left few faculty members in positions to challenge her authority and tenure was unheard of.

The strike, called by faculty members who formed an association, lasted for most of the school year. Millicent McIntosh, then

---

[36] Lloyd, op. cit., p. 129.
[37] Ibid., p. 129.

Dean of Barnard College and a Putney parent, was called in to mediate in Spring 1949. Although there is disagreement as to just how much the strikers accomplished, salaries were raised, tenure was granted after 3 years, and faculty workloads and obligations were specifically delineated. Governance of the school was to be shared by an administration council, which would consist of four faculty members named by the principal, three faculty members elected by classroom teachers, and one faculty member elected by the farm staff. Additionally, 20 teachers formed The Putney Teachers Union of Public Workers, CIO Local #808.

Ultimately, the Putney School settled on a plan for shared governance, modeled on the one adopted by Antioch College. Hinton was committed, according to its historian, Susan M. Lloyd, to demonstrating that her school would be run cooperatively. Nevertheless, the history of Putney once again demonstrates the paradox present in progressive education: Although schools founded on Deweyan principles sought to create democratic communities, their leaders too often presided over their creations autocratically. The Putney School was particularly important in the history of progressive education for, as Theodore Sizer noted, "It was a piece of the last, great flowering of progressive school building."[38] Furthermore, the Putney School, although child-centered, attempted to create a community that would serve as "a microcosm of a better, more democratic world [in which] the lives of schooling education, and life were to be erased . . . [nevertheless, was] autocratically led."[39] Hinton went further than either Pratt and Parkhurst, because she created a community for adolescents in which they would learn and work together. It was a bold experiment in living and learning and it is a tribute to Hinton that her vision of progressive education still exists.

CONCLUSION

Caroline Pratt, Helen Parkhurst, and Carmelita Hinton founded progressive schools that were both child-centered and micro-

---

[38] Ibid., p. ix.
[39] Ibid., p. ix.

cosms of democratic group life. Their schools represent the early ideas of Dewey on democracy and education rather than the more radical ideas of the reconstructionists, who saw schools as instruments of specific social reforms. What is particularly perplexing about these models as presented here is the style of leadership exhibited by these female founders, which is frankly autocratic, in stark contrast to the ideological thrusts of the schools they founded.

Perhaps the examples of these female founders suggest that to have accomplished what they did, they needed to possess both clearly articulated philosophies of education and the will to implement them. Given the politics of education of the period, it is not likely that female school heads and especially female pedagogical pioneers would have succeeded if they had been more democratically disposed. Indeed, history suggests the opposite.[40]

Recent studies of women and leadership suggest a style of female manager very much at odds with the examples of Pratt, Parkhurst, and Hinton. For example, books such as Sally Helgasen's *The Female Advantage* and articles such as Judy B. Rosener's "Ways Women Lead" suggest that women manage very differently than men; that women naturally form *centiarchies*— nonhierarchical organizations with the leader at the center rather than at the top—in contrast to the male hierarchical ones with top-down management. Rosener, in particular pointed out that there are several important characteristics of female leaders such as encouraging participation, sharing of power and information, and enhancing the self-worth of others.[41]

These theories are controversial and continue to be hotly debated, in particular by sociologist Cynthia Fuchs Epstein who stated, "Even if people are putting women on a pedestal now, it's still mindless aggregation. The notion at the base of this debate is that women have a single personality that doesn't capture the rich variation in people."[42] Nevertheless, the idea of female leadership with its "web of inclusion," although lacking empirical data, is gaining in popularity. Although this chapter cannot begin to address current thinking about female leadership as

---

[40] David Tyack and Elisabeth Hansot, *Managers of Virtue* (New York: Basic Books, 1982), Chapter 5.

[41] Judy B. Rosener, "Ways Women Lead," *Harvard Business Review* (November–December, 1990), pp. 119–125.

[42] Jaclyn Fierman, "Do Women Manage Differently?" *Fortune* (December 17, 1990), p. 116.

creating webs of inclusion, it can point out the danger of attempting to impose current ideas about female leadership on examples from the past.

Pratt, Parkhurst, and Hinton were creations of their time and place. They were visionaries and innovators and were determined to create, from their visions, tangible results. That they did so, often autocratically, often forcefully, speaks more to what may be required of women involved in innovative, creative experiments. Ultimately, their creations—City and Country School, The Dalton School, and The Putney School—transcend the issue of gender and remain monuments to their particular progressive visions and their force of will in implementation and administration. They present an interesting paradox to scholars of democratic education, and should be judged, as philosopher William James might have suggested, "Not by their roots but by their fruits."

6

SOUTHERN PROGRESSIVISM DURING THE GREAT DEPRESSION: VIRGINIA AND AFRICAN-AMERICAN SOCIAL RECONSTRUCTION*

Michael James
Connecticut College

For many of us, the Great Depression of the 1930s is captured in the photographs of Dorothea Lange; images of squalor and despair, the dirty scuff-grays and somber moods of poor whites and destitute blacks; innocent faces that seemed to tolerate the present as they looked to some distant future with little

---

* This chapter is part of a larger comparative work on the history of civil rights and schooling in two regions: the far West and the South. This chapter was supported, in part, by a summer 1992 fellowship at the Virginia Foundation for Humanities and by the generous travel stipends provided by the R. Francis Johnson fund at Connecticut College.

hope.[1] In the large cities, bread lines and Hoovervilles, violent strikes, and payless paydays mocked a nation that to millions of native-born and immigrants alike had been God's Promise Land. But it was the hopelessness of rural, backwoods poverty that was so poignantly conveyed in Lange's images as she wandered the depressed countryside. In the South, to sharecroppers white and black, to laborers, section hands, and generally the poor and working class, the depression of the 1930s brought havoc to an already impoverished landscape. Like the "Great War" it followed, this holocaust was to be forever cursed by its victims as the Great Depression, a cuttingly ironic description of a decade of revolution that changed the world.

If the Great Depression was hard on poor whites, it was harder still on Southern blacks. Caught in a culture of seemingly inescapable poverty that grew out of a rigidly segregated social system, Southern African-Americans during the depression apparently had few choices: Either live within a biracial society or leave. All over the South, African-Americans voted with their feet as outmigration was one form of social protest.[2] Throughout the Black Belt states, thousands abandoned the land and headed to cities in the North and West. In Virginia, as an example, the rural black population continued to fall throughout the first three decades of the 20th century, whereas the numbers of urban African-American dwellers during that same period remained fairly constant.[3]

---

[1] Under the guidance of no one and drawing funds from Roosevelt's Farm Security Administration, photographers such as Lange, Marion Post Wolcott, Ben Shahn, Russell Lee, and Jack Delano drove the highways and backroads of the country documenting the ravages of the depression. For Lange, it was an opportunity to have her work alleviate some of the suffering. Apparently it did, as she and the sociologist Paul Taylor's documentation of migrant workers led to government camps. See David P. Peeler, *Hope Among Us Yet: Social Criticism and Social Science* (Athens: University of Georgia Press, 1988), pp. 57-58; *Dorothea Lange*, with an introductory essay by George Elliott (New York: Museum of Modern Art, distributed by Doubleday, 1966).

[2] See *The Great Migration in Historical Perspective: New Dimensions of Race, Class, and Gender*, Joe William Trotter, Jr. (Ed.), (Bloomington: Indiana University Press, 1991), especially his Introductory Essay, pp. 1-21 and Earl Lewis, "Expectations, Economic Opportunities, and Life in the Industrial Age: Black Migration to Norfolk, Virginia, 1910-1945," pp. 22-45; Nicholas Lemann, *The Promised Land: The Great Black Migration and How it Changed America* (New York: Alfred Knopf, 1991).

[3] As an example, in Albemarle County, in which Charlottesville was the only incorporated city, from 1910 to 1920 the overall (white and African-American)

To the African American, the much heralded New South of the 20th century was merely another version on the old: Poverty for most was constant as everyone endured a segregated society that socialized whites and blacks into believing their world was preordained to be divided by color and class. This biracial state was nowhere more apparent than in Southern schooling, where since the end of Reconstruction, children had attended schools decided by the color of their skin. In Virginia, by the turn of the century, African-American children were educated almost universally by black teachers, and in nearly every black school in the state, black men served as principals and administrators.[4] Always though, educational policy for "Negro Schools" in Virginia, as in every Southern state, was controlled by whites.

Throughout the South, the *Plessy* "separate but equal" ruling was seldom if ever equal. African-American children attended schools that were woefully underfunded and understaffed, with equipment and supplies that were often nonexistent, and a school year that was nearly always shorter than their white counterparts. Education for Southern African-American children was, as historian Carter Woodson wrote early in the decade, "mis-education."[5] With the coming of the Depression, what had served as education for black children would be severely curtailed; school terms would be further reduced and teachers' salaries cut to a point where many in rural schools would earn significantly less than half of what their white colleagues earned

---

county population declined by 3,866, yet the city of Charlottesville grew by nearly the same number due in part to annexation as well as rural outmigration. 2,104 African Americans left the county during the same period and increased the city population by 423. See *The Negro in Charlottesville and Albemarle County: an Exploratory Study*, Marjorie Felice Irwin, University of Virginia, Master's thesis, published by the Phelps-Stokes Fellowship Papers in 1929.

[4] See James Anderson, *The Education of African-Americans in the South, 1860–1930* (Chapel Hill: University of North Carolina Press, 1988). Regarding African-American administrators and teachers in Virginia, see J. Rupert Picott, *The History of the Virginia Teachers Association* (Washington, DC: National Education Association, 1975), p. 72 for a discussion on white teachers in black schools in the late 19th century and the *Bulletin* of the Virginia State Teachers Association, Vol. *10*(3), May 1933, p. 4 on the Richmond Board of Education finally giving in to VSTA pressure to allow African Americans to secure administrative positions in the city's black schools, a practice long urged by VSTA and apparently practiced throughout most of the state. The statement on school administrators being "black men" needs no additional commentary; typically women did not administer schools in Virginia.

[5] Carter Woodson, *The Mis-Education of the Negro* (Washington, DC: Associated Publishers, 1933).

in the cities. All over the region, as communities responded to the economic crisis, white and black schools alike—but more often the latter—hit bottom and closed their doors.[6] Politicians talked of sacrifice and in communities all over the country teachers responded. In Virginia, the State Superintendent told a back-slapping, self-congratulatory Assembly in May 1933 that the success in keeping an 8-month term was due more to teachers staying on even as the money ran out rather than the solvency of the State Treasury.[7] Teachers could not, though, in Virginia and elsewhere, continue to carry the schools. As despair deepened, the mood of many turned to a mix of rage and hope: for both African Americans and whites, working-class, middle-class, teachers, and tenant farmers, there was a sense that something was about to change.

PROGRESSIVE EDUCATION AND THE GREAT DEPRESSION

By the winter of 1932, millions were out of work and to the no-longer-working men and women in cities and small towns all over America, there apparently was little President Hoover would, or could, do about it. Paydays came and went without paychecks being issued. For those who had jobs, salaries were cut 10%, 20%, 30%, or more. People lost their homes, banks seized farms or farmers simply walked away, abandoning the family lands that had been worked for generations. Money seemingly vanished overnight as banks and savings institutions were forced to lock their doors. Children left school by the thousands in a futile attempt to find work somewhere, anywhere. Three years after the panic of 1929 it appeared to many that the country

---

[6] See David Tyack, Robert Lowe, and Elisabeth Hansot, *Public Schools in Hard Times* (Cambridge, MA: Harvard University Press, 1984), p. 32 for comments on school closings all over the country.

[7] See *The Richmond News Leader*, May 25, 1933, pp. 1,3. In Red Hill, a small community not far from Charlottesville, the white school board closed two black schools, transferring the funds and one teacher to another black school in an effort to save money. This kind of consolidation is discussed in Tyack's *Public Schools*, pp. 188, 201–203. For a description of Red Hill, see William Leap's *Red Hill*, University of Virginia, Master's thesis, published by the Phelps-Stokes Fellowship Papers in 1929.

was dangerously close to economic Armageddon. The hard and fast rule of capital and cheap labor producing wealth—and jobs—had turned to myth: How could this land of plenty, with its rich and abundant natural and human resources, suffer such misery? From progressives and the socially elite to those in bread lines and on the family farm there was a growing resentment toward what Sinclair Lewis called the "monied aristocracy" and a laissez-faire economic system that promoted conspicuous consumption, extravagant wealth to the few, and selfish individualism.

As the depression worsened, well-known, mainly Northern educators who for a generation had relied on a child-centered, progressive pedagogy to frame their cultural agenda, joined with the political and social left to articulate a series of far-reaching, radical proposals to ameliorate the tensions that existed between the American liberal tradition and the lure of Marxian economic systems that seemed to offer some release from the vicissitudes of capitalist declines, booms, and busts. Calling themselves social reconstructionists, educators, philosophers, and social critics including Sidney Hook, John Dewey, William Kilpatrick, Boyd Bode, and George Counts (who had just returned from the Soviet Union to see for himself if the proletarian revolution was real), advanced the notion that teachers and the work they perform should aid in easing the crisis.[8] The reconstructionists believed the crisis had been exacerbated because schools, both child-centered and traditional, public and private, reflected the moribund values of a class-bound society bent on self-protection at all costs. Counts, in his now famous *Dare the Schools Build a New Social Order?* wrote in 1932 a biting condemnation of the middle class:

> They [the middle class]. . .possess no deep and abiding loyalties, possess no convictions for which they would sacrifice over-much, would find it hard to live without their customary material comforts, are rather insensitive to the accepted forms of social injustice . . . and in the day of severe trial will follow the lead of the most powerful and respectable

---

[8] See C.A. Bowers, *The Progressive Educator and the Depression* (New York: Random House, 1969), as well as James Giarelli's analysis of the reconstructionist journal, *Social Frontier*, in this volume.

forces in society and at the same time find good reason for doing so.[9]

To the reconstructionists the principal aim of schools and teachers should be to prepare individuals, as Kilpatrick wrote in 1933, to "take part intelligently in the management of their lives, to bring them an understanding of the forces which are moving, and to provide them with the practical tools with which they themselves can enter into the direction of these forces."[10] Kilpatrick's definition of cultural reconstruction called for an educational system that functioned at the cutting edge of social change, rather than reacting in knee-jerk fashion to successive crises, oblivious to the larger cultural voices of status quo and reaction. What the educational reconstructionists and a wide array of socially progressive intellectuals wanted schools to do was take the lead in reshaping culture away from the hierarchical notion so embedded in 20th-century industrial capitalism. Schools and teachers then would participate equally in a cultural redefinition of America: a collective society dependent less on the wealth of the few and more on the planning of the many. The social reconstructionist agenda cut at the very nature of how America thinks about culture and order, and threatened the very definition of power and who governs.

For those bent on reclaiming what they believed was a more democratic culture, these early years of the decade were heady times. Radical forces were at work; revolutionary ideas were capturing the imagination of workers, farmers, African-Americans, the young and old alike. In the South, the early years of the decade invited, as George Tindall wrote, "radical agitation."[11] Communists and trade unionists in the cities organized industrial and textile workers and in the countryside the Share Croppers' Union was formed chiefly among poor whites and African Americans. All over the region, there was "desperate but nebulous talk of revolution."[12] Even the self- proclaimed patriarch of a reactionary and racist South, Governor Theodore Bilbo of

---

[9] George S. Counts,"Dare Progressive Education Be Progressive?" *Progressive Education*, 9 (April, 1932), p. 258.

[10] See William H. Kilpatrick, *The Educational Frontier* (New York: Appleton-Century-Crofts, 1933), p. 71.

[11] See George Tindall, *The Emergence of the New South, 1913-1945* (Baton Rouge: Louisiana State University Press, 1967), p. 385.

[12] Ibid., p. 385.

Mississippi, told reporters in 1931 that "folks are restless ... communism is gaining a foothold ... I'm even getting a little pink myself."[13] Bilbo's assessment of communist gains—and his political coloration—are far fetched; yet the economic base of a progressive New South was nevertheless seriously threatened by the depression. By 1933, fully one third of the region's railroads were in receivership, farm profits had all but disappeared, and financial institutions both at the state and local level were ill-equipped to deal with the crisis.[14] State revenues continued to dry up and that meant in Virginia, as throughout the South, fewer dollars for schools.

It is ironic that in the midst of this great economic and social catastrophe, when both white and black schools were subject to gross underfunding and the very fabric of Southern society was unraveling,[15] African-American educators in Virginia made their greatest gains in the struggle against inequality and segregation. By seizing the ideology and language of the social reconstructionists, African-American educators in Virginia were able to carve out for themselves a tenuous foothold in state educational policymaking. What makes the study of Virginia education—both black and white—during the 1930s so ironic, is that social reconstruction, with its themes of radical community change being initiated by a vanguard of teachers liberating the masses and creating a "new kind of society," was never intended for African Americans. Furthermore, at least in Virginia, the very idea of social reconstruction may have been for whites merely a transitory illusion, for the ideals of progressive community rebuilding appear to have been more a conservator of the status quo than a mechanism for radical democratic change.[16]

---

[13] Ibid., pp. 385–386, cited in Hilton Butler's "Bilbo-The Two-Edged Sword," in *North American Review*, CCXXXII (1931), p. 496.

[14] Tindall, pp. 365–367.

[15] William Link, *The Paradox of Southern Progressivism, 1880–1930* (Chapel Hill: University of North Carolina Press, 1992); George Brown Tindall, *The Emergence of the New South, 1913–1945* (Baton Rouge: University of Louisiana Press, 1967).

[16] See Ronald Goodenow "Paradox in Progressive Educational Reform: The South and the Education of African-Americans in The Depression Years," *Phylon* (March, 1978).

RECONSTRUCTING VIRGINIA

Progressive pedagogy and the idea of a socially reconstructive educational system came to Virginia when Sidney Hall was appointed State Superintendent of Public Instruction in 1931.[17] A native Virginian and former Director of Secondary Education in Richmond's State Department, Hall was at the time of his appointment on the faculty of George Peabody College. Knowing Hall's public and very progressive views on educational change and knowing further the reticence of Virginia's political establishment to invest much—either funds or liberal ideas—in schooling, Hall's appointment appears at first blush to be contradictory.[18] In the private correspondence between Senator Harry Byrd and his lieutenants, it is clear Hall's appointment came with strings attached. The Democratic party in Virginia controlled state politics and Harry Byrd controlled the party. Hall was a dark-horse candidate, and only when the leading candidate withdrew at the 11th hour, did Byrd agree to Sidney Hall.[19] During the early years of the decade, Hall repeatedly told Byrd that he could deliver the state's teachers, but at a cost. For

---

[17] Hall's appointment was announced just before the new year, 1931; see the *Charlottesville Daily Progress*, December 30, 1930, and the *Virginia Journal of Education*, January 1931. There were "progressive" ideas being discussed during the late 1920s by William Smithey's University of Virginia-based secondary administrators organization, but it was not until Hall, a longtime friend of Smithey, came to the office of Superintendent that any real effort was made to reorganize practice around the state; for information on the secondary education movement in Virginia see *The Virginia Teacher*, the conference proceedings of the High School Conference held annually at the University of Virginia beginning in 1921.

[18] For comments regarding Hall's appointment, see Herbert Kliebard, *The Struggle for the American Curriculum, 1893-1958* (London: Routledge & Kegan Paul, 1987), pp. 223-227; Barry Franklin, *Building the American Curriculum: The School Curriculum and the Search for Social Control* (London: Falmer Press, 1986), pp. 127-131; Mary Louise Sequel, *The Curriculum Field: Its Formative Years* (New York: Teachers College Press, 1966), p. 173; Michael James, "Schools and Cultural Change—Retrospect and Prospect: The Virginia Curriculum Revision Project, 1931-1941," *The National Social Science Journal*, 1(5), (Spring, 1990), pp. 13-24; Lynn Burlbau, *Hollis Caswell: An Intellectual Biography*, Doctoral dissertation (University of Texas, 1989).

[19] The *Charlottesville Daily Progress*, expressing sentiment that seemed to typlify attitudes around the state, commented "the appointment of Dr. Hall to become the state's educational leader came as a distinct surprise to educational circles as well as the general public" (January 30, 1930, p. 1).

the next decade Hall and Byrd struggled over who was to control the state's educational machine. In the end, it was to be Byrd.[20]

Hall was an astute politician who envisioned himself as president of some major university. There was speculation throughout his tenure as Superintendent that he was about ready to jump ship for William and Mary, Peabody, or even the University of Virginia.[21] A persuasive public speaker, Hall was enigmatic, handsome, energetic, and from the very first days of his appointment, clearly the one in charge, as much as anyone could be with the Byrd Organization looking over his shoulder. He believed the ideals of a progressive New South—science, efficiency, industry, and democracy—would free Virginia from the old ways of waste, ignorance, political cronyism, and paternal-

---

[20] See the correspondence between Byrd, Hall, and E.R. Combs, one of Hall's closest advisors, in the *Harry Flood Byrd Papers, Alderman Library, University of Virginia*, 911–1965,(Acc 9700) Box 116, Box 140, Folders: "Sidney B. Hall," 1930-1933, 1933-1936, and Box 93; Folder: "E.R. Combs," 1930. Hall was clearly one of the Organization's staunchest supporters but he was equally adamant that Byrd support the schools during the crisis. More than once he let Byrd know that the teachers were solidly behind the Organization, but if the Minimum Education Program, which was Hall's plan for revitalizing public education, was not passed then he was in no position to guarantee anything. He pleaded with Byrd to support the schools, and if he would: "Your name would not only be remembered for your great achievements as Governor, but that you would more than ever be remembered as the individual who helped save the schools. . .for the State in the most serious crisis which we have ever experienced." (Hall to Byrd, January 9, 1933).

[21] In a letter William Smithey wrote to Hall when he was teaching at Peabody, he encouraged Hall to try for the presidency at Fredericksburg. Hall later told Smithey he did not feel the time was right "to enter the scramble for Fredericksburg." Not long after Hall took over as State Superintendent, the *Richmond News Leader* reported that he was in line for the superintendent of Richmond's schools. Later in the decade his name was repeatedly mentioned as a candidate for president of William and Mary, Peabody, and once, University of Virginia. See Hall to Smithey in the *William Royall Smithey Papers, Alderman Library, University of Virginia*, [acc RG-21/54.801;861], folder: "Correspondence: 1928-1929"; see *The Richmond News Leader*, May 20 and 24, 1933 for commentary on the city superintendency; for speculation on Hall leaving for a college presidency, see the *Richmond News Leader*, August 21, 1935, and the *Richmond Times-Dispatch*, July 17, 1936. Regarding Hall leaving for William and Mary, historian Richard Sherman of William and Mary believes Hall was passed over for the presidency in 1934 just because he was "a school man." There was concern that the institution, which had a rocky financial and intellectual base, would be perceived as a teacher education college if Hall was appointed. The Trustees instead turned to the aging John Stuart Bryan. See *John Stuart Bryan*, unpublished biography by Douglas Southall Freeman, in *Virginia State Historical Society*, Chapter 16, for comments on Bryan's presidency. Sherman's comments came in a telephone conversation with the author.

ism.[22] His was an educational enterprise that would not only equalize school funding, systematize a haphazard bureaucracy, improve teacher pay and retirement, but most important, redesign the very experience of school. In the spirit of true progressivism, education would bring Virginia into the 20th century. He understood, though, that any fundamental change in school experience would necessitate changes in educational governance. Reforming schools in Virginia would require the building of coalitions and it would begin with the most powerful professional organization in the state, the High School Principals Association. By 1932 the Virginia Curriculum Revision Project, with the enthusiastic blessing of most administrators in the state, was underway.[23]

Logistically the Project was spread over eight Curriculum Centers: the University of Virginia, the State Teachers Colleges and Virginia State College for Negroes at Petersburg, the center set aside for curriculum design for the state's entire African-American school population.[24] The State Department at Richmond asked each of the institutions to recommend a committee of local talent to monitor the creation of new curricula, ostensibly to be designed through the input of some 12,000 to 15,000 classroom teachers as they worked in study groups all over the state during 1931 and 1932. In reality, the form of revision was in place long before the workers, who have been characterized as the real force behind this revision, ever got to their study groups. What has been characterized as a grass-roots, teacher-led, statewide reform effort was in reality the creation of a small

---

[22] For an excellent analysis of the social policies of the New South see William Link, *The Paradox of Southern Progressivism, 1880-1930* (Chapel Hill, NC: University of North Carolina Press, 1992); as well as Edward Ayer, *The Promise of the New South: Life After Reconstruction* (New York: Oxford University Press, 1992).

[23] See the many articles and editorials in the *Virginia Journal of Education*, the white teachers' association magazine. Hall's first speech was before the high school administrators. Hugh Sulfridge, principal of Lane High School in Charlottesville and president of the Virginia Education Association, believed Hall's plan brilliant and "no greater importance could claim our attention." See the *Virginia Journal of Education*, 25(3), (November, 1931) for coverage of the Annual Convention in Richmond. The theme of the convention was "Curriculum Revision." Hall's first public meeting was with the high school principals where he discussed his 14-point plan for reconstructing education in Virginia.

[24] In addition to University of Virginia, the centers included Fredericksburg, Radford, Harrisonburg, Farmville, William and Mary, and Virginia Polytechnic Institute.

group of men, most notably Hollis Caswell from Teachers College, who served as Hall's curriculum consultant, and Frederick Alexander, chair of the Aims Committee.[25] More to the point, it was Alexander and Caswell who probably wrote the project's guiding Aims during the summer of 1932.[26]

As the revision program unfolded, it was clear that the language of school reform in Virginia was democratic, participatory, liberating, cooperative, and reconstructive.[27] Caswell, who we believe was the real architect of the program, idealized a "Democratic Man," his vision of the activist-citizen whose education had prepared him to be responsive to society's ills. Caswell had come to believe that social ills were the result of what he called "disordered social functions." Schools can aid in the correction of social functions by introducing early in a child's education a set of key ideas, "woven," as one curriculum historian would write later, "right into the child's performance."[28] Knowledge of function creates processes of control, thought Caswell. Formal education, then, could take the lead in the reconstruction of culture.

This educational and culturally reconstructive process, however, needed guideposts: central, functional ideas classroom teachers might employ as they wrote units of study. These organizational structures were the "aims, understandings, and generalizations" that Alexander and Caswell wrote during the summer

---

[25] See Hall's introduction to the *Bulletin* of 1932 in which he commented on Alexander et al., *Procedures for the Virginia State Curriculum Program*, (Richmond, VA: State Board of Education, 1932).

[26] See Lynn Burlbau's "More Than Ten Thousand Teachers: Hollis Caswell and the Virginia Curriculum Revision Program," *Journal of Curriculum and Supervision*, 6, (Spring, 1991), pp. 233-254, for an analysis of the process. Alexander and Caswell worked during the summer on the aims; the others on the committee turned the work over to Alexander, but no reason was given. It may have had to do with funds.

[27] See the "Hollis Caswell Interview" by Tom Hogan, *Columbia University Oral History Project* (1969), p. 107. In a oral history interview conducted at Columbia, Caswell called the aims "radical," and "controversial." He was interviewed later by O.L. Davis of the University of Texas and commented that the aims were, again, radical and controversial. In the Davis interview, though, Caswell disavowed any connection between the Virginia program and Counts' ideas on reconstruction. See Hollis L. Caswell, Interview by O.L. Davis, Jr., October, 17, 1977 (Tape Recording, Oral History Collection, *Center for the History of Education*, The University of Texas at Austin).

[28] See Mary Louise Sequel, *The Curriculum Field: Its Formative Years* (New York: Teachers College Press, 1966), p. 173.

of 1932. What was created for Virginia were some of the most far-reaching and radical educational ideas to come out of any statewide revision program. Alexander admitted that he had tried to answer George Counts' call for a reconstructive America, as the guidelines he created gave the revision program, at least on paper, a decidedly anti-big business bent. Alexander suggested teachers design curriculum around generalizations such as "Individuals and powerful minorities have always sought to control and to subjugate," and as a result, "Many of the significant movements of history have been caused by man's effort to throw off the yoke of oppression and slavery." Democracy, then, should be seen as "a new thing in the world, as an experiment in the effort to establish human rights for all men." Because the theoretical base of progressivism had broken with absolutism, Alexander wanted teachers to instill in their students the idea that "The present social order is not fixed and permanent. Man continues to modify it in search for justice and freedom." To some, especially those in the African-American community, these were ideals to be taken seriously. Later the notion of a reconstructed social order would come back to haunt both Hall and Alexander.[29]

As far as big business and laissez-faire capitalism were concerned, Alexander offered as aids for curricular innovation a collection of provocative themes. Educators and their students should understand that "The material prosperity of the modern world has been attained under the capitalistic system," but, Alexander cautioned, "Capitalism is based on the principle of profit to the owner rather than to service to the masses of the people." As a result, then, "The distribution of goods in a capitalistic society tend to direct social products into the hands of the few." If teachers were aware that "Production is based on the amount of goods purchasers can be induced to consume, rather than upon their needs," then they would understand that "The capitalistic system is not planned and lacks direction thus waste and economic cycles result." Alexander concluded by telling teachers that "The dependence of the laborer upon capital tends to reduce him to a servile status."[30]

---

[29] *Bulletin*, pp. 16–17, 24–26.
[30] *Ibid.*, pp. 24–26.

In an article he wrote in 1934 for the *Clearing House*,[31] Alexander went so far as to infer that the avant garde ideals of the revision program could be at work in Virginia's junior and senior high schools. He rather subtly suggested his essay was an "interpretation" and an "example of the role of these major functions of social life in the Virginia course of study," but the message was clear that here were concrete ideals promoting social revolution. High school students involved in the revision program, he wrote, could be "discussing ways in which the church, the school, and the press restrict thinking and conduct to bring out the ways in which you are denied the intellectual and social freedom that you should have." They might be "arranging bulletin board[s] showing how the press tends to interfere with the realization of the democratic ideal." Students could be "visiting courts and industrial plants and interviewing laborers, lawyers, and people who have been convicted of crimes to learn in what ways the poor and nonconformists are deprived of justice." Materials, said Alexander, were carefully selected so they "present a well-balanced discussion." Alexander concluded that subject matter was used to broaden the pupils' "experiences through engaging in socially useful activities that will enable him to realize attitudes and understandings that he can use in managing and re-creating a new kind of society."

This was a curious essay, for Frederick Alexander was no radical; he was well connected to the Newport News business community and never established himself as being left of center in his political or educational views. His daughter believed he was a political independent, but tended to vote Democratic.[32] As principal of Newport News High School he was known by students and faculty alike as an authoritarian, a "no-nonsense administrator," as one of his former students, now a retired U.S. Congressman, described Alexander's administration. When faculty saw him walking down the hall with a stack of books tucked under his arm they wondered aloud if they were about to experience a 30-minute or 3-hour meeting. When he was appointed Director of Negro Education in 1936, he quickly established himself as a conservator of the biracial status quo rather than a moderate looking toward change. His authoring of aims

---

[31] Frederick Alexander, "Social Studies in Virginia," *The Clearing House*, 9(2), (October, 1934), pp. 76–81; Michael James, "Frederick Alexander," *Virginia Dictionary of Biography* (Vol. 1, Virginia State Library, Richmond, in press).

[32] James, "Frederick Alexander."

that were decidedly anticapitalist, anti-Church, and near-Marxist in language if not intent, indicate perhaps that he had been swept up by the drama of Counts' culturally transformative ideology. In the early days of the decade, when talk of revolution and reform were laced throughout both the popular and educational press, Alexander might have believed what he wrote. His *Clearing House* essay was carefully crafted to emphasize the most revolutionary, antiestablishment aspects of the revision program. If he did not believe in the ideals of social revolution, then why did he single out those activities that had students "interviewing school officials, ministers, and newspaper editors to determine their part in building a new social order?"[33] Then again he might have believed that the teachers of Virginia would never take seriously the more radical aims of the revision program. If that be the case, then his contribution to the revolutionary literature of the old left has a cynical, hollow ring, written no doubt to further his career rather than as inspiration for social change.

As far as can be determined from newspapers, interviews with students and colleagues, and the extant correspondence, what Alexander wrote about education being socially reconstructive occurred in theory only; nowhere can it be found that white schools used the revision program to remake their communities.[34] It is reasonable to think that Hall, Caswell, and Alexander expected the less controversial content would be put into practice around the state, and to an extent, it was. Subject integration, what educators called *core work*, was experimented with in schools all over the state. Hall told James Johnson, Superintendent at Charlottesville, that Waynesboro, Radford, Matthew Whaley High School in Williamsburg, and Creadock High School in Norfolk were "some of the more sanely progressive schools" engaged in core work.[35] What Hall meant by "sanely progressive"

---

[33] Alexander, p. 81.

[34] See the James biography of Alexander for citations and source notes. The *Virginia Journal of Education* had numerous articles with titles suggesting reconstructive content, such as "The Schools and the New Social Order," but overwhelmingly these essays prove to be commonplace. For comments on Alexander's role as Director of Negro Education, see the William Mason Cooper Papers at Hampton. Cooper was an officer of the Virginia State Teachers Association and later president of Virginia Union University.

[35] Sidney Hall to James Johnson, April 12, 1940, in *The Charlottesville School Board Papers, The Papers of Albert G. A. Balz,"* mss 3795, Box 1, Folder "1940 Curriculum Committee: Lane High School (new white High School)." Balz

is unclear but there is little evidence to suggest Alexander's aims of revolution were operating anywhere in white schools around the state. What is clear is that the leadership in Richmond never expected the African-American community would seize for their own use the program's reconstructive ideals.[36]

AFRICAN-AMERICAN RECONSTRUCTION

It became clear as the revision project got underway that regardless the language of reform, the project never intended to democratically reconstruct the inequities in Southern society. When D.W. Peters, Director of Instruction at the State Department, asked President John Gandy of Virginia State College to recommend a committee to oversee the design of school-based materials, it was evident whites envisioned something different for African-American children. The College was to serve "as a center for all work in the state which involves any special adaptations that may be proposed for Negro Children."[37] Gandy and his faculty were furious; "special adaptations" could mean only one thing: a curriculum designed to further segregate, in this instance, by substantiating through school practice the fallacy that intelligence was colorbound. For the last 15 years, African-American educators and social scientists had argued long and well that educational performance could not be predicted by intelligence testing.[38] Gandy's faculty saw "special adaptations" as further proof that their arguments had fallen on deaf white ears.

---

was president of the Board in the late 1930s and a member of the philosophy department at UVa.

[36] See the O.L. Davis interview of Caswell in which he states, in effect, that African-Americans were not interested in the revision program.

[37] See the correspondence between Gandy and Colson, in *The Colson-Hill Family Papers, 1834-1984*, (acc. 1965-13), Virginia State University Archives, Petersburg, VA, Box 65, Folders: "VSU correspondence with John Gandy, 1930-1931," 463 and 464, "1932" January 25, 1932, October 24, 1932, November 1, 1932.

[38] See the many articles in the *Journal of Negro Education, The Virginia State Bulletin, and The Southern Workman,* all relating to the inequality of intelligence testing, viz. African-American intelligence and children.

John Gandy, for 30 years patriarch of black education in Virginia, asked Edna Colson, a young professor of elementary education at the College, to recommend an Advisory Committee to answer the State Department.[39] Colson, working on her doctorate at Teachers College under George Counts and Mabel Carney, assembled a group of some of the brightest and most progressive educators in Virginia. Among her selections was a young colleague, Doxey Wilkerson, since 1927 Director of the High School Program at the College. It became evident immediately that he was a brilliant and politically passionate young man who understood the nexus between race and social class. His early writing was often about choice and the power that comes from community organizing.[40] Later in the decade he would leave Virginia for Howard University, serve on Roosesvelt's education Advisory Committee, then in the early 1940s, as vice president of the American Federation of Teachers (AFT), join the Communist Party, edit Harlem's weekly *People's Voice*, teach at the Jefferson School for Social Science in New York, and finally at Yeshiva University. Throughout his career he was attacked by whites for his turn to communism, but black Virginians never lost their

---

[39] Colson to Gandy, November 1, 1932. Colson and Gandy had already organized a committee to study curriculum development long before the State Department request. In a letter dated January 7, 1931, she recommended to Gandy a list of names for a revision study group. The staff from the College agreed that the revision process would be difficult, at best: "What there is of value not included in the bibliography is so likely to be of equal difficulty, that we recommend such organization of study groups as will provide the most able leadership available and extension of time for those who are slow of comprehension." She recommended William Cooper from Hampton, Winston Douglass from Richmond, Eva Mitchell from Hampton, L.F. Palmer, principal from what would later in the decade be the most progressive African-American high school in the state, Huntington High School in Newport News, and Archie Richardson, who in 1936, would be appointed by Hall to the State Department as Assistant Director of Negro Education. Cooper, Douglass, and Palmer would serve as VSTA presidents and later college presidents; Mitchell would serve as Director of Research during most of the 1930s.

[40] See his many articles in the VSTA *Bulletin*, and the *Journal of Negro Education(JNE)*, especially his analysis of the African-American tobacco workers' strike, which won the right to organize and higher wages, which appeared January 1938 in *JNE*. In that study, he compared the tobacco workers' wage increases to the wage of an African-American Virginia teacher. See the VSTA *Bulletin*, November 30, 1930, April, 1931, January 19, November, 1932, March, 1933, January, 1934, March, 1935, as examples.

admiration for Wilkerson and his lifetime of work to equalize educational opportunity.[41]

Wilkerson and Colson were to become the catalysts for much of the reconstructive material to come out of Virginia during the depression. Wilkerson believed one of the greatest impediments to African-American education was a system of social relations that created a sense of dissolution, despair, and futility. He often used the parable of a dog who, bound for years by a fenced yard, was unable to see the open gate.[42] It was through schools that Wilkerson and other African-American progressive educators saw the open gate: Teach young children that they had the power to reconstruct their world; teach them that their world was not limited but that through struggle and planning, they could make this "new kind of society" that Alexander had alluded to.

It was evident from the outset that Wilkerson, Colson, and the Advisory Committee intended to use the progressive rhetoric of the Virginia Curriculum Revision Project for purposes different than what Richmond intended. In Colson's words, the Committee "launched itself into a course of study" that within a year would result in a brilliant rebuttal to the State Department's request for "special adaptations."[43] Symptomatic of a separate and unequal social system, Richmond paid little attention to what African-American educators wanted or needed to accomplish their task. Throughout the revision process, Colson complained frequently and at times bitingly that Peters and his staff were slow, vague, noncommittal, and above all else, unresponsive to "the needs of the Negro."[44] Frustrating as this was, in a sense they were left to

---

[41] Wilkerson was criticized by Wilson Record in his polemic on communism and African-Americans, *The Negro and the Communist Party* (Chapel Hill: University of North Carolina Press, 1951). Closer to home, Blair Buck, who came to the State Department in the late 1920s from Hampton and later would be appointed Director of Instruction, wrote in his unpublished autobiography that Wilkerson, no matter how Buck tried to talk him back into the fold, had thrown it all away by joining the CPUSA. He, like Record, referred to Wilkerson's years with the CPUSA as "a waste." See Michael James, "Blair Buck" in the *Virginia Dictionary of Biography* (Richmond: Virginia State Library, Vol. 1, in press). A copy of the autobiography is in the author's possession. Wilkerson died in June 1993 in Norwalk, Connecticut. See his obituaries in the *New York Times*, June 18, 1993, and in the Norfolk, Connecticut, *The Hour*, June 18, 1993.

[42] Interview by author with Sam Madden, July 29, 1992, Petersburg, Virginia.

[43] Colson to Gandy, October 24, 1932.

[44] Colson to Gandy, September 15, 1934, March 4, 1935; Colson to Ruth Henderson, November 22, 1935, April 5, 1935, February 5, 1936. Colson also criticized the State Department in the VSC *Gazette*, December 1933, pp. 1–5, and in a

their own resources and they responded accordingly. Some 9 months after the initial call for revised materials, Peters requested his first meeting at Virginia State College to "discuss the things Negro teachers can do in the State Curriculum Project." Gandy, the Committee, teachers, principals, and Jeanes Supervisors all met to hear Peters, who showed up so late for the meeting he could only make a brief comment or two about the need for "understanding...the nature and function of the curriculum by the average classroom teacher" and "the proper organization of . . .materials considered especially important in the education of the Negro."[45] It was the latter set of instructions about procedures that apparently impressed Wilkerson and the Committee. Knowing how the State Department would respond to any attempt to attack Jim Crow directly, Wilkerson, in a June 1933 letter, cautioned curriculum makers throughout the state to follow precisely the procedures the State Department prescribed; no use having their efforts thrown out by a technicality.[46] In mid-August, after Peters paid a second visit to the College, the Committee sent their work to Richmond and then in December, published the same in the College magazine, the *Gazette.*

The Advisory Committee rejected any notion that curricular adaptations were necessary because of "inherent racial differences in intellectual ability or special aptitudes." Then Wilkerson and the Advisory Committee departed significantly from prior arguments:

> Curricular adaptations because of race can justifiably be proposed, then, only in the light of social problems which result from racial factorfs. [sic] If there be such problems, it seems to follow that they represent social needs which make demands upon education, needs to which special curricular adaptations should be made.[47]

---

letter to Charles Thompson, editor of the *Journal of Negro Education,* January 31, 1934, pp. 2-3. Wilkerson was struck by Colson's ability to attack without apparent fear of reprisal. In a letter to Colson he wrote he "wishes he had the gift for saying bitingly pertinent things diplomatically, inoffensively, though none the less forcefully. I have in mind the first and last paragraphs of the letter to Mr. Peters. Do tell me of his response." See Wilkerson to Colson, from Ann Arbor, December 2, 1933. Wilkerson was in Ann Arbor working on his doctorate.

[45] Virginia State College *Gazette,* 3B(4), (December, 1933), p. 5.
[46] Ibid., p. 4.
[47] Ibid., p. 6.

Any social problems come as a result of the nature of a biracial state, not as a result of some misguided idea that intelligence was colorbound. Accordingly, "the approach of education in meeting these needs, therefore, must also be bi-racial." If social problems that result from segregation are to be solved by education, then the Committee reasoned, schools of both races should be involved in any solution. Wilkerson and the others had effectively turned the revision program on its head. Along with the "Basic Philosophy" that rejected differences in racial intelligence, the Committee laid out 15 social problems that call for "special adaptation in the curriculum of all children," including political problems, racial stereotypes, problems of health, economics, crime, and delinquency. The Committee sent Richmond a set of "guiding aims" calling for a common course of study, inclusion of reconstructive materials in teacher education, model units, a comprehensive bibliography, and a program of study for the secondary schools on African-American education that is remarkably similar to what today might be termed an Afrocentric curriculum.[48] Above all, Colson stressed that "the materials lose their significance when the philosophy of education which justifies their use is not understood."[49]

The Advisory Committee understood the significance of what they had done; after Colson had given Peters the Committee's statement and the materials, she told Gandy it was "a momentous occasion."[50] She was optimistic that Richmond would incorporate their views when the Tentative Course of Study for Elementary Schools was published in September 1933,[51] no doubt because Peters had assured her the State Department would include their materials. The State Department had no such intentions; the Course of Study carried the following comment about African-American education Colson termed "unfortunate": "The Committee for Negro schools suggests units of work in connection with the aspects of the several centers of interest that will be especially valuable in Negro schools." The State then listed the themes the Committee intended for all children as if they were to be used exclusively by African-American schools.

---

[48] Ibid., pp. 12–17.
[49] Colson to Charles Thompson, January 31, 1934, p. 3.
[50] Colson to Gandy, July 19, 1934.
[51] On July 19, Colson to Gandy. She advised Gandy that they had met with Peters and the meeting was a "momentous occasion. . . we hope our offerings will be properly incorporated in the forthcoming bulletin of the State Department."

For the next 3 years African-American educators, especially Colson and her colleagues at Virginia State, worked to have their viewpoint included in official State Department *Bulletins*. No matter Peters' assurances that what they produced would be published, the State Department continually either altered or omitted the Committee's position on how best to achieve the New South in Virginia.[52]

What Wilkerson, Colson, and the Advisory Committee had written was more than an answer to Richmond: It was a call for African-American social reconstruction through education. The Advisory Committee and the scores of black teachers who participated in the revision program used the language of progressive reform to attempt to remake their communities: African-American history and music; studies of voting and nonvoting patterns in the black community; home life; health; studies of African-American educators, scientists, and inventors; studies of black poetry, religion, and folk life; readings on village life in Africa, the colonization of Africa, the Civil War in America, and slavery and its consequences in Virginia during the 1930s; internal migration and its reasons during the 20th century—all these were topics not merely proposed by higher education faculty for use in African-American schools. Many were incorporated in teacher-designed units for use in classrooms throughout the state, intended to be used by both white and black students. Colson and her colleagues at Virginia State, the Hampton Institute, and Virginia Union were in schools on a regular basis working with teachers designing and implementing progressive and reconstructive curricula. From mid-decade on, faculty and students participated in a series of community surveys, gathering data on demographics, health, housing, economics, and voting patterns. The surveys were apparently utilized by Luther Jackson, professor of history at State when he formed the Virginia Negro Voters League in the early 1940s.[53]

By the end of the decade, the State Department had become aware that the reform process instituted by Hall and guided by

---

[52] See Colson to Thompson, January 31, 1934, and Colson to Henderson, November 22, 1935, February 5, 1936.

[53] Colson to Gandy, October 11, 1935, November 14, 1935 for her annual reports on how the department was aiding the development of the "new curriculum." Also see Goodenow's "Paradox in Progressive Educational Reform: The South and the Education of African-Americans in The Depression Years," *Phylon* (March, 1978).

Alexander's aims was contributing to a reconstructed definition of civil rights. Teacher study groups had formed to examine and evaluate the status of African-American education within the context of an overall, statewide assessment of the revision process. There were over 200 African-American study groups in 42 counties and in nearly every city that was asked to participate. Study Conferences were planned at three regional centers including Virginia State College. The groups had begun to discuss, among a wide-ranging set of problems and issues, civic participation, an idea antithetical within a segregated society and apparently so odious to certain local officials that the State Department had the study groups and conferences canceled.

Even so, one observer noted that the groups and conferences had "made the Negro more conscious and dissatisfied with his educational plight," something not intended by the original revision process or the late-decade evaluation.[54] Virginia's African-American community continued to push, pressure, at times chide and confront Jim Crow over issues that were vital to the quality of life in the African-American community. The Advisory Committee, through its work and the work of countless black teachers did more to turn progressive theory into practice than did progressive white educators anywhere in the South. The number, scope, and especially the reconstructive content of articles published in the *Bulletin* far exceeded what appeared in the *Virginia Journal of Education*, the white teachers' association magazine. Moreover, the work of the Advisory Committee marked the beginning of a new era in African-American political power in Virginia.

THE POLITICS OF EDUCATION IN VIRGINIA

Sidney Hall appears to have had little direct contact with the revision process other than by educating audiences about the virtues of curriculum reform as he traveled the state. Rather, what consumed Hall throughout the decade was keeping schools open full term, diluting the effects of the depression on budgets—

---

[54] See Archie Richardson, *The Development of Negro Education in Virginia, 1831–1970* (Richmond, VA: Phi Delta Kappa, 1976), p. 52.

especially his own—and feuding with Harry Byrd as he tried to prod an unmoving Assembly to fund his Three-Point Plan: an average minimum salary, improved retirement, and free school textbooks.[55] Extremely active in the national arena—Hall was an editor of the *Social Frontier* as well as Chair of the National Education Association (NEA) Legislative Committee—the Superintendent by the end of the 1930s was one of the most politically powerful educators in the country. Perhaps realizing the futility of pushing for increased funding from the Virginia Assembly, as well as sensing the changing mood of the Congress during Roosevelt's second administration, Hall threw his energies into securing federal aid for schools.

By the winter of 1936–1937, there appeared to be enough support on Capitol Hill to pass legislation granting large sums of money ($300 million within a few years) to states to assist in equalizing educational opportunity. Initially, however, this was not money intended to equalize white and black schools in the South; instead, equalizing educational opportunity was an NEA-sponsored bill to bring poor and wealthy states into some balance. The NEA lined up support for the campaign, including what they thought was tacit approval from the White House.[56]

In addition to the expected conservative political and religious antipathy to federal aid to schools, by the early spring of 1937, as hearings were being held, a new coalition, led by the American Federation of Teachers (AFT) and the NAACP, demanded significant changes to the bill.[57] As the bill was drafted, there were no provisions to guarantee that federal money would not be used disproportionately by Southerners to perpetuate the inequality between white and black schooling. The AFT/NAACP opposition

---

[55] See the correspondence between Hall and Byrd in the *Harry Flood Byrd Papers* at University of Virginia, especially Hall to Byrd, January 14, January 30, June 16, December 13, December 15, 1932, and Byrd to Hall, December 12, 14, 1932 and June 18, 1932. In a letter Hall wrote in January 1933, he told Byrd that he was having difficulty keeping the teachers "in line"; the fiscal crisis and Byrd's reluctance to support the teachers' needs apparently were causing Hall to openly criticize the organization (Hall to Byrd, January 26, 1933). He told Byrd that he did not want the next General Session to be like the last where "only after serious difficulties that I was able to keep the school organization in line."

[56] See Anne Gibson Buis, *An Historical Study of the Role of the Federal Government in the Financial Support of Education*, Doctoral dissertation (Columbus: Ohio State University, 1953), pp. 213–283.

[57] Marjorie Murphy, *Blackboard Unions: The AFT and the NEA, 1900–1980* (Ithaca, NY: Cornell University Press, 1990), pp. 131–149. Murphy mistakenly has Hall coming from West Virginia.

to the unamended bill was problematic. Both organizations knew Southerners would never support federal aid with strings attached, especially if those strings somehow dictated to states where federal dollars were to be spent. Yet, the NAACP and AFT were not opposed to federal aid; on the contrary both organizations recognized the need—the AFT had sponsored a rival bill that not only included safeguards sought by the NAACP but allocated more money. If the legislation, known as the Harrison–Black–Fletcher bill, was to go forward it needed support from the AFT and NAACP as well as other African-American and labor organizations.[58]

As chair of the NEA's Legislative Committee, Hall had worked closely with Willard Givens, NEA's executive secretary, and John Studebaker, Roosevelt's Commissioner of Education. He had met personally with the President, extending a 5-minute interview into 15. He was optimistic that there was a growing resolve on both sides of the aisle for federal aid. He knew the fragile nature of coalition building, and knew better still how quickly this opportunity might evaporate. Roosevelt was not about to support any legislation that might damage his Southern alliance and any bill requiring that federal funds be color blind might alienate Southerners from future New Deal legislation.[59] The President's inherent distrust of "school-people," as he referred to public educators, further clouded the issue and made the timing of the bill crucial.[60]

Indicative of Hall's political power and ambition, but more likely because of NEA concern that their efforts might go awash, he chaired the week-long House hearings, calling before the Committee on Education a series of speakers to buttress not only

---

[58] Ibid., pp. 146–149; Gilbert E. Smith, *The Limits of Reform: Politics and Federal Aid to Education, 1937–1950* (New York: Garland Publishers, 1982), pp. 56–60.

[59] Smith, pp. 56–57; Murphy, pp. 141–149; Andre R. O'Coin, *Vocational Education During the Great Depression and World War II: Challenge, Innovation, and Continuity*, Doctoral dissertation (University of Maryland, 1988), pp. 265–296. He mistakenly has Hall as NEA president, pp. 283, fn. 79; see Martha Swain, *Pat Harrison: The New Deal Years* (Jackson: University Press of Mississippi, 1978), pp. 210–218 for an excellent analysis of Harrison's role in federal school aid legislation.

[60] David Tyack, Robert Lowe, and Elisabeth Hansot, *Public Schools in Hard Times* (Cambridge, MA: Harvard University Press, 1984), p. 107.

the NEA position but to blunt AFT/NAACP opposition.[61] The NEA and Hall could not control the testimony of African-American leadership, such as Charles Thompson of Howard or Charles Houston of the NAACP, but Hall could show the Committee that not all African-American educators were against the bill as it was written. Hall placed on the calendar two African-American Virginians. One was T.C. Walker, a conservative Richmond attorney who for years had influenced the Negro Organization Society, a community-based school support group that later merged with the state's PTA. Walker countenanced no controversy and no opposition to the white-controlled school system in Virginia. "Discriminations," said Walker, "have always existed, but there is no need of advertising them; we think the best way of getting rid of them is by taking no notice of them." He told the committee, "this bill, it appears to me, is a God-send to the school system of Virginia and to the school systems of the whole country so far as the Negro people are concerned." Walker concluded by assuring Hall and the Committee that "there are some things we have to be mighty careful about in this matter; we do not want to excite in any of your activities anything that would bring about race friction."[62]

Following Walker, Hall brought Archie Richardson, the first African American to be appointed to Virginia's State Department of Education. Richardson's praise for the Harrison bill was gushing; he repeatedly called for passage of the bill without amendments:

> We should like very much to see this bill passed. We feel that to earmark the bill in its present stage of development may defeat the purpose of the bill. . . .We feel that [to do so] is chal-

---

[61] *Hearings Before the Committee on Education House of Representatives*, 75th Congress, 1st Session, HR 5962. To promote the general welfare through the appropriation of funds to assist the states and territories in providing more effective programs of public education (March 30, 31, April 1, 2, 6, 8, 13, 1937). Hall presided over the House hearings and arranged the calendar for both the Senate and House hearings.

[62] *Hearings Before the Committee on Education and Labor United States Senate*, 75th Congress, 1st session on S. 419 (February 9–11, 15, 1937), pp. 216–219. See Elizabeth Cobb Jordan, *The Impact of the Negro Organization Society on Public Support for Education in Virginia, 1912–1950*, Doctoral dissertation (University of Virginia, 1978), for a discussion on Walker's views of schooling.

lenging the honestly and integrity of the white people in Virginia.[63]

Richardson's testimony, largely constructed from Booker T. Washington's accomodationist philosophy, led him to argue that in Virginia "if you want honey, you do not kick over the beehive." He went on to tell Hugo Black, Senator from Alabama:

> I believe that the future success of the Negro lies in his intelligent cooperation with the most intelligent leaders of the white group, and that by resorting to any drastic action, we are simply raising red flags that give the other group an opportunity to strike back and possibly wound more seriously.[64]

To the Committee, Richardson's Virginia was one of compromise, cooperation, fairness, and opportunity. In all respect to his tenuous position as Assistant Director of Negro Education, to keep his job Richardson would have been hard pressed to advocate anything other than the Hall party line. No doubt his comment about "intelligent cooperation with the most intelligent leaders of the white group," was in reference to his boss, who was sitting directly in front of him. Richardson did not volunteer nor did the Alabama Senator ask, but the newly appointed Assistant Director, when he returned to Richmond, would return to a segregated State Department building so ill equipped to deal with a black male that Richardson had to relieve himself in the basement, bring his own lunch to eat alone in his office, or leave the building to lunch at a local diner. A few years later when Hall appointed his second African-American administrator, Sam Madden, WPA Director of Vocational Education for Negroes, the State Department denied him an office in Richmond and sent him to Hampton.[65] As far as the aid legislation was concerned, the 4-year NEA-sponsored campaign went for naught; Roosevelt refused to support funding if it would jeopardize his Southern alliance, which apparently it did as a result of the AFT/NAACP effort to amend the Harrison bill.

---

[63] *Hearings*, pp. 222–227. Although he does not mention his appearance, see Archie Richardson's historical sketch, *The Development of Negro Education in Virginina, 1831–1970* (Richmond: Phi Delta Kappa, 1976).

[64] *Hearings*, p. 226.

[65] Richardson, p. 50; author's interview with Madden.

The bill was dead for the meantime, but out of the campaign the NAACP and AFT had significantly enhanced their ability to serve as power brokers within national politics.[66] And in Virginia, African-American educators, as a result of publicly confronting Hall and his choice of witnesses, were able to broker a new political reality for themselves.

Hall's political gamesmanship on the Hill had backfired. When it was reported that Richardson, and to a lesser extent Walker, had spoken as if for the entire African-American community—their repeated use of "we" was perhaps intentional—the outcry from the African-American press, not only in Virginia but nationally, embarrassed and angered Hall.[67] It is highly unlikely the Superintendent was so naïve that he failed to understand that Walker and his own State Department employee were speaking for themselves rather than the majority of African-American educators; Hall's anger and embarrassment more likely came as a result of his inability to believe that the African-American community would contradict his position. Whatever the wellspring of Hall's motivation, he had been exposed; his efforts to represent Virginia and by implication the entire South as a united, cooperative, biracial front had collapsed. Opposition to the bill within the African-American community was solid and the NEA and Hall were forced to back down at substantial political cost. More to the point, not only had Hall's witnesses become suspect, but during the hearings, representatives from the Virginia State Teachers Association publicly refused to back the Harrison bill.

Hall was furious, but according to William Cooper of the Virginia State Teachers Association Legislative Committee, the Superintendent was "now interested in the Association in a new

---

[66] Murphy, p. 149

[67] See the editorial in the *Journal of Negro Education* (April, 1937), pp. 131–132, written by Charles Thompson. He cited numerous editorials in national weekly newspapers that were critical of Hall and his "'hand-picked' Negroes from Virginia," as one editorial sarcastically informed its readers. Thompson quoted a letter from Gandy written the day after Richardson's appearance in which he criticized supporters of the bill and in a pointed reference to Richardson's "intelligent Negroes" comment, Gandy wrote: "I think I know the sentiment of the intelligent Negroes of Virginia very well, and I would unhesitatingly bear witness to the fact that in my opinion they do not approve of the Harrison–Black–Fletcher Bill as drawn." He concluded that "We do not know anything about the appearance of the two Virginia witnesses before the Committee in the interest of the Harrison–Black Bill."

way."[68] Once back in Richmond, Hall ordered Frederick Alexander, now Director of Negro Education, to set up a meeting between himself and the VSTA. Alexander told the Association's leadership, made up of many of the same individuals who had served with Wilkerson and Colson on the revision project, that Hall wanted to "get together with our group."[69] Cooper, from the Hampton Institute, was selected to meet with the Superintendent. According to Cooper's notes, a somewhat aloof Sidney Hall, reaffirmed "without any personal feeling" that his position on the Harrison bill should have been accepted. No doubt sensing his changing political fortunes, and too smart to let this opportunity pass, Hall asked the leadership of the African-American teachers association to form a committee to "act with the Virginia Education Association" and, personally, for the VSTA to select "someone to whom he [Hall] might turn to find out the attitude of the Negro teachers in such matters."[70] Candidly, Cooper told Hall that "they too had been embarrassed," and from this newly won position of strength, he went on to tell Hall that if they had only been consulted from the beginning they would not have had "to go against him."[71] Cooper did not tell us how the meeting ended, only that the Superintendent sent him down the hall to the Virginia Education Association office where he was given ballots to send "thru-out the state," probably to secure African-American opinion on federal aid. For the first time, African-American teachers in Virginia had secured a toehold in Virginia politics. Cooper referred to the meeting as a first "cooperative effort" between white teachers and the black educational community. That community's newly won political power would quickly lead to tangible gains as Hall and the Virginia Education Association would drop from the Three-Point Plan the term *average* when referring to a minimum salary. By 1939, the Three-Point Plan referred simply to a "minimum salary of $720." [72]

---

[68] See Cooper's comments in the *Virginia Teachers Association Papers, Executive Secretary Record Books*, acc.#0069-14 Box 1 (November 13, 1937).
[69] Ibid.
[70] Ibid.
[71] Ibid.
[72] Ibid. See the *Virginia Journal of Education*, 33(1), (October, 1939), which makes no mention of average. The issue of salary equalization was first mentioned by Gandy in 1919 and throughout the 1930ss VSTA had actively worked to have "average" removed from the Three-Point Plan.

Cooper's notes were made while he was in executive session at the November 1937 Richmond meeting of the VSTA. At that same meeting was Thurgood Marshall, NAACP attorney, who told the committee and then later the entire Association of his and the NAACP's appreciation of the stand the Association had taken on the Harrison–Black–Fletcher bill. Marshall told them that the "[House] Committee learned exactly the position of the Southern Negro on this bill."[73] Marshall was there not only to applaud the Association for its stand on federal aid, but to report on the court battle in Maryland over salary equalization. By the early 1940s, building and enlarging on their political base, Virginia's African-American teachers would lead the fight for equalization as the Supreme Court would affirm in the *Alston* case that the Norfolk Board of Education could not pay equally qualified black teachers less than whites.[74]

THE DEMISE OF SIDNEY HALL

Salary litigation would be the final chapter in Sidney Hall's professional career. His repeated run-ins with Byrd's Democratic Organization over issues of money and power repeatedly placed him outside the machine. Apparently his ongoing feud with Byrd also placed him outside the Organization's protective cover, for amid rumors of possible scandal involving his personal life, he resigned during the summer of 1941 to become Director of Continuing Education at George Washington University in Washington, DC. When he announced his resignation, which had been leaked to the press while he was away in Florida, he told the educational community that his work in Virginia was done and he wanted to return to a more tranquil life in higher education. The Richmond press, though, smelled a story and reported that the capitol was "uncharacteristically closemouthed."[75] When the

---

[73] Ibid.

[74] Ibid.; Mark Tushnet, *The NAACP's Legal Strategy Against Segregated Education, 1925–1950* (Chapel Hill: The University of North Carolina Press, 1987), pp. 78–80, 102–103. Marshall, claimed Cooper, was not there to recruit salary litigants.

[75] *The Richmond News Leader* and *The Richmond Times-Dispatch*, August 12, 1941, p. 1.

Richmond Times-Dispatch asked the Governor to comment, James Price refused, yet when Hall returned to the capitol he contradicted Price and told reporters he had "acted with the Governor." The Superintendent's "retirement" as he referred to his departure, remained shrouded even as Hall was packing his bags. Days later Price still refused to comment. This lack of closure by the Governor, either words of praise or damnation for a state leader with a national reputation, only tended to mystify an already confusing affair. The last the *News Leader* would write about Hall came a few days later when the paper concluded, "He has already transferred his interests in property on Seminary Road to his wife, Mrs. Stella R. Hall. The deed of bargain and sale was filed in Henrico County on August 8." [76]

It remains unclear why one of the most respected educational leaders in the country left his seat of power at the height of his influence to assume an obscure position in continuing education. Hall may have tried to strike some kind deal with Byrd's liberal Democratic Party opponents in Price's administration, or he may have become expendable to Price just because he would not cooperate with Virginia's new Democratic liberalism. The fact remains, however, that no matter where Hall stood in relation to Price and his group, good friends of the Organization do not suddenly walk away, left professionally penniless. Almost from the day of his resignation, Hall became persona non grata: Educators around the country knew his name, but he no longer was a force in national educational debate. His work at NEA dried up during the war years, probably due to the nature of his position at George Washington. He no longer had any political base; it was as if he had been banished from the kingdom.

RECONSTRUCTING VIRGINIA

Hall's departure did not hamper the movement within the African-American community to remake Virginia. By the end of the 1940s it was clear that the slow pace at which Jim Crow had

---

[76] *The Richmond News Leader* and the *Times-Dispatch*, August 14, 1941, p. 1. The *Virginia Journal of Education*, 35(1), (September, 1941) quoted Hall as saying he had accomplished much and therefore, "felt free to return to university teaching" (p. 3).

been under attack since the turn of the century was quickening. The all-white graduate and professional schools had been forced to accommodate African-American students, the University of Virginia was now accepting both African-American graduate students and women as undergraduates, and salaries between whites and blacks had been equalized. The pedagogical promise long associated with progressive education—child-centered instruction, less reliance on textbooks and more on exploration and discovery—may have been less important to progressive African-American educators than teaching young children the history and culture of the African and African-American. It was that legacy—self-knowledge and the power of education—that is the essence of social reconstruction in any community, white or African American. The effort by black educators like Edna Colson, Doxey Wilkerson, John Gandy, and countless others to reconstruct African-American Virginia helped create a foundation that served to buttress what we have come to call the civil rights movement.

7

SOCIAL RECONSTRUCTIONISM FOR 21ST-CENTURY EDUCATORS

William O. Stanley III
Largo, FL
Kenneth D. Benne
Boston University

Many contemporary students of educational philosophy in America write about schooling and social policy as if no philosophy named social reconstructionism, both by its proponents and its opponents, thrived in discussions of educational policies for America only a few decades ago. References to social reconstructionist journal articles and books, plentiful in the 1930s and into the 1970s, are meager or missing in current discussions of the purposes, the organization, and the methods of educational effort that are most apt to the waning 20th century. All these aspects of education were treated freshly and distinctively in the literature of social reconstructionism.[1]

---

[1] We refer, as social reconstructionists, to published studies of education by such scholars as George Counts, the later John Dewey, John Childs, Karl Mannheim, Harold Rugg, R. Bruce Raup, Theodore Brameld, the early B. Othanel Smith, William O. Stanley II, and Kenneth D. Benne, among others.

Widespread neglect, if not ignorance, of this recently productive emphasis in educational philosophizing in America (and in Great Britain, too) is ordinarily justified in one of three ways. The reconstructionist recommendation that educators should aim to transform our political economy is often dismissed as hopelessly utopian, as a timebound and "emotional" response to the Great Depression of the 1930s and to the totalitarian regimes and inhumane holocausts that stemmed from decadent capitalism at that time. Secondly, social reconstructionists' consistent advocacy of participative democracy in planning, living, and learning to live, in schools and out, are countered by assertions of the alleged inevitability of pyramidal organization of human effort in efficient decision making and management of enterprises involving large numbers of people and requiring the services of various specialized experts. Bureaucratic organization is said to be inescapable whether the enterprise is privately or publicly owned and operated. Decisions, on this view, must be taken from a limited number of places in society and by a limited number of powerful and specially trained personnel. Finally, social reconstruction may be dismissed as not being "philosophical" at all, because it does not conform to strictures that the later Wittgenstein placed once and for all on the "philosophic" enterprise. Philosophers must leave that which they analyze unchanged.

We argue to the contrary. We hold that global participative planning of the use or nonuse of technologies in the future (if there is to be a future for human life on earth) and the reorganization of human collectivities, private and public, into nonbureaucratic forms are both possible and desirable. Deep cutting and continuing education and re-education of both persons and collectivities are, we believe, necessary in converting the unstable and violence-prone oligarchies in which we now live into democratic planning societies. Philosophy for us, as it was for William James, is an effort to think as deeply and critically as possible about the practical (moral and political) problems faced by contemporary men and women as they live into an uncertain future. It is not unphilosophic for philosophers to recommend changed normative outlooks to their contemporaries.

There are both continuities and discontinuities between social reconstructionist diagnoses of our political economy and their recommendations to educators as these views surfaced in America in the 1930s, and the social reconstructionist views we are recommending now. Social reconstructionist thinkers have consistently advanced three basic propositions about the best way to orient educational effort in the continuing and deepening crises that characterize postmodern societies and cultures.

INTERDEPENDENCE

The first is that widening interdependence and the erosion of local self-sufficiency stem from dependence on "humanly" uncontrolled and profit-driven markets to direct the flow of investments in capitalist economies. Individual or corporate owners act primarily to maximize self-interest. They must focus their attention on the short-range consequences of their economic choices and actions. With interdependence growing to global proportions, market operations by themselves are increasingly inadequate to take account of and to assess effectively the long-term costs and benefits of economic ventures and exchanges.

Early social reconstructionists emphasized such phenomena as the persistence of poverty and joblessness in a world of potential plenty, the persistent unavailability of low- and medium-cost housing and health care to many, the oppression of masses of people, the humanly punishing vagaries of the business cycle, and the omnipresent threat of fascism as undesirable effects of primary dependence on market operations to steer and control our political economy. They were, for the most part, unaware of the limits to economic growth set by the maintenance of a viable, life-friendly environment on earth.

Today, we must also emphasize the deepening ecological crisis that now confronts people around the globe. It is widely recognized that ecological problems involve a marked discrepancy between private costs and social costs. For example, in an unregulated market economy, firms that pollute the water and air do not pay the full cost of their actions because many costs are incurred and paid for at a considerable distance in both space and time from the actions themselves. Moreover, the costs to a firm of its own polluting acts may be seen as negligible because they are small when compared with combined polluting acts from many other sources. So long as other firms continue to pollute, it may be profitable for owners and managers of any one enterprise to continue to pollute, however severe the long-term economic, social, and personal costs to other and all human beings, including polluters themselves, may be.

There are, of course, many current threats to a viable earth—the continuing dangers of nuclear holocaust, global warming, a depleting ozone layer, ravished wetlands, and runaway genetic engineering are now evident to many educators, though the evidence seems not to have affected markedly the thinking of educational reformers about the required content, method, and clientele of teaching and learning in and out of schools.

Neoconservatives who worship guidance by an unseen hand in market operations tend to see ecological threats as requiring only sporadic and uncoordinated interventions by a bureaucratized state, by well-crafted televised images of concern about "the problem" that emanate from the headquarters of multinational corporations, and by the development and use of new technologies to offset the abuses of polluting technologies. This last is analogous to the development of anti-anti-missiles to offset dangerous fallout from antimissiles designed to defend against missiles. and so on, ad infinitum. Leaders in economic, governmental, and educational circles do not typically speak of changed human ways of thinking, valuing, and controlling personal and civic conduct as basic to the maintenance of a viable earth. We, as educators, must do so.

Social reconstructionists see the need for participative planning, local to global, in optimizing the benign and curtailing the malign uses of older and of newly emerging technologies. Such planning, to be effective, will require changes in modes of human thinking and conduct, habits of consumption, and authoritative socioeconomic norms and policies. As Benne argued, personal morality must be politicized and politics moralized.[2] Reconstructed educational and re-educational policies and programs and radical redeployment of services by educators will be required. We must learn to live as friends and allies, not conquerors, of the earth.

Social reconstructionists in the 1990s do not call for the elimination of modern technologies or of continuing efforts to develop new technologies. They call for novel and imaginative uses of the technologies of communication and information processing now available. And they urge that public investment

---

[2] Kenneth D. Benne, "Toward a Moral Basis for Politics and a Political Basis for Morality," *Educational Foundations*, 5(2), (Spring, 1991).

in scientific and technological research be shifted from a focus on weaponry with its accompanying limitations on open sharing of research and developmental results in the name of national security or competitive advantage. They insist further that comprehensive, global, social planning, much of it local in focus, of the use or nonuse of technologies and, as a consequence, of priorities in capital investment, must replace the profit motive as the chief or primary determinant of economic undertakings. There are natural limits to mindless economic and population growth.

PARTICIPATIVE DEMOCRACY

The second fundamental belief of social reconstructionists has been a commitment to participative democracy as the only satisfactory way to create and maintain legitimate and authoritative normative principles and policies in human collectivities, whatever their size or population. Democracy, for the reconstructionists, is not primarily a plebiscitary way of periodically electing officials or of ratifying plans prefabricated for them by some distant elite. Rather, democratic community is needed in order to attain and maintain legitimate norms in all social and economic organizations, including educational institutions, as tradition direction declines and as conflictive traditions need to be reconciled and new traditions created, as Benne argued throughout the half century just passed.[3]

One reconstructionist argument for democracy is that a once competitive and free market with many small producers and distributors has come to be dominated by giant corporations, often multinational and conglomerate in character, and so beyond effective control by any national government, regulatory agency, or professional association. These socially irresponsible corporations have the power to set and administer prices and to distort free market competition. Such concentrations of economic power in the hands of a few, with limited accountability to

---

[3] See Benne, "The Meaning of Democracy in a Collective World," In Kenneth D. Benne, and Steven Tozer (Ed.), *Society as Educator in an Age of Transition* (Chicago: National Society for the Study of Education, 1987); Kenneth D. Benne, *A Conception of Authority* (New York: Russell & Russell, 1943).

the many persons and peoples whose lives are affected by their decisions and actions, have led to the control of contemporary societies, including our own, by only nominally democratic oligarchies. Most reconstructionists recognize that a state bureaucracy can be as unaccountable and socially irresponsible as a private corporation when it is not subject to open criticism and control by its citizens. We argue for the eventual institutionalization of participative social planning over all the earth. Significant social and cultural changes under the direction of such an ideal set Herculean tasks for postmodern re-education.

THE POLITICS OF CULTURE

The third fundamental assumption of social reconstructionists is that the economic and political systems of a people must be distinguished from but are, nevertheless, closely interrelated to its normative culture. A crisis in political and economic systems also means a crisis in culture. Unsolved problems in an economic system conceivably could be understood and remedies for the problems worked out by qualified experts without joint deliberation with those who must enact the solution—the workers. But a crisis in normative culture can be understood and worked through only with the communicative participation of actors who give life to the culture by their willing acceptance and uncoerced affirmation of the legitimacy of its norms.

Dealing with the contemporary ecological crisis can help clarify the meaning of this claim. Political action and economic planning, involving the participation of various experts and professionals, is required to attain and maintain a viable environment on earth. But such action and planning will not suffice without accompanying creation of ecologically sound norms and ideals by persons who are active and communicative participants in today's human cultures, whatever their expertise or lack of it. Because cultures are diverse, cultural transformation must be achieved by communicative participation across cultural boundaries. The implication of this view for adequate programs of education and re-education are profound.

The crisis in valuation that now plagues our lives requires further diagnosis to develop the fuller meaning of the three basic beliefs of reconstructionists in the 1990s. An internal critique of Karl Mannheim's[4] diagnosis of our time provides a good starting point for the exposition of our own views.

KARL MANNHEIM

Mannheim began with a narrative, identifying three stages in the story of socioeconomic development in the West. These strategies are marked by the scale and character of interdependent effort involved in socioeconomic innovations and by the extent of reliance on deliberate human interventions in instituting such innovations.

Most of human history, at least in the West, belongs to the Age of Discovery. Socially inherited traditions were dominant in giving direction and pattern to methods of producing, distributing, and consuming goods and services and to various forms of life. Calculation and deliberate human intervention played a much less important role than they have come to play in developed or modernized societies. Innovation depended on chance trial and error or success of sporadically conceived novel ways of doing or interpreting things. Most persons lived in relatively autonomous, economically self-sufficient, and closely knit local communities. Individuals were socialized and enculturated (educated) into a customary round of life through face-to-face communication and participation. There were, ordinarily, large-scale pyramidal organizations—religious, secular, or both—in the background of village and rural life. Hierarchical organization of differentiated specialist roles characterized the courts of kings, popes, pashas, and suzerains. Far-flung markets operated in the exchange of exotic goods, but these systems penetrated far less deeply into the ongoing lives of most people than they do today. Interventions into local life were made mainly in the levying of taxes or tributes, drafting manpower into military service, and the appointment of priests.

The next stage Mannheim referred to is the Age of Invention, which was a far shorter period, historically speaking, than its

---

[4] See Karl Mannheim, *Man and Society in an Age of Reconstruction* (New York: Harcourt Brace, 1950).

predecessor. It refers roughly to the period following the medieval (and perhaps the mercantilist) centuries in Europe. In this age (an age in which some neoconservatives seem to believe that we are still living) private "enterprisers" came consciously to innovate in economic affairs on a wide scale.

Max Weber linked the heightened incidence of entrepreneurial ventures in Europe with widespread acceptance of the individualist Protestant ethic.[5] As communitarian views yielded to individualist views of human conduct, each entrepreneurial unit pursued his or its (rarely her) own self-interested objectives. Little conscious attention was given to the coordination and regulation of various private ventures and innovations. At the same time, larger networks of interdependence developed at the expense of local self-sufficiency. In the economic realm, coordination was effected by market operations. Imbalances due to discrepancies between supply of goods and services for sale and the effective demand for them were corrected after the fact by changes in market prices. This is an example of what Mannheim called *spontaneous adjustments*, on which people in this age depended for coordination of multiple and scattered linear developments. The market solution with its recurring periods of boom and bust was viable because local self-sufficiency survived in some degree in village and rural life, enabling people to live through the cyclical shocks of market dislocations.

Important changes in culture occurred as the age of spontaneous adjustments in economic life progressed. Local community life, patterned by uncriticized socially and religiously sanctioned customs, was undermined. Face-to-face communication and participation in processes of personal socialization, social integration, and cultural reproduction (for us these are names for different aspects of basic educational processes) became more difficult. In the language of Habermas, the economic system was uncoupled from the life worlds of Western peoples.[6] Their life worlds were increasingly rationalized, but rational alternatives to the once tradition-controlled processes of integration, socialization, and reproduction were not institutionalized effectively to control the often inhumane and antihuman effects of a socially irresponsible economic system. Modern equivalents to tradition-directed

---

[5] Max Weber, *The Theory of Social and Economic Organization* (London: Oxford University Press, 1947).

[6] Jurgen Habermas, *Theory of Communicative Action: A Critique of Functionalist Reason* (Boston: Beacon Press, 1987).

local communities as agencies of basic socialization were sought, but none survived except those that placed religious boundaries around their way of life—the Amish in America, for example. Hundreds of Owenite, Fourierist, and other planned communities were established in America during the mid-19th century. This is evidence of the widely felt need for a planned community life, as socially irresponsible processes of industrialization and urbanization progressed. It gives evidence also of the power of capitalist institutions to survive at the expense of community by perpetuating popular myths—in America, those of inevitable progress and of the American Dream—myths now cankered by doubt and disbelief.[7]

More recent evidence of the need for community in the "lonely crowd" of advanced capitalist societies may be found in the emergence of thousands of support groups in the population of developed countries. These are contrived to provide mutual nurturance to individuals beset by various wounds, troubles, and yens—alcoholics, persons with heart transplants, parents without partners, epileptics, gamblers, philatelists, and believers in witchcraft among many others. One difference between contemporary support groups and 19th-century planned communities may reveal something about the depth of despair or the height of hope about the achievement of significant general social change that characterizes 19th- and late-20th-century Americans. Fourierists, Owenites, followers of John Humphrey Noyes at Oneida, or of Bronson Alcott at Brook Farm, hopefully believed that they were pioneering a model way of life that might spread through the greedy, "getting and spending" society from which they were recoiling. Support groups today typically have no social mission. They are designed to protect minority individuals who differ in some way from those in the ruling majority—a majority often unfriendly to those who are different. Perhaps they might be rallied into coalitions to modify the prevailing negative orientation of the majority toward deviance, if they

---

[7] The undermining of traditional ways of social integration is, of course, a threat to the continued dominance of power elites. As a society becomes more interdependent, disruption of coordination at any point tends to spread through the system. Concentration of decision-making power in a few key positions makes the holders of these positions more heavily responsible for the maintenance of the system. The undermining of traditional ways of social integration reduces the ability of the ruling elites to control the behavior of mass populations in emergencies when control is most crucial.

might, through re-education, acquire hope about their potency to change their own minds and the minds of others.[8]

Mannheim's Age of Invention was thus characterized by linear thinking, random innovations in the economic sphere, and dependence on spontaneous adjustments (often reified as "natural") to rescue human societies from the periodic dislocations into which their thinking and practice led them. Political and economic leaders paid limited attention to the consequences of changing life conditions for human culture and for the general quality of life. *Quality of life* has tended toward a deeply misleading identification with *standard of living*.

Dependence on market operations as the principal steering mechanism in capitalist societies has deprived persons and families of the wider social support once provided by tradition-directed local communities. The conversion of rooted villagers into a mobile mass is the result of such deprivation. Mannheim's recommendation of social planning was in part motivated by his recognition of people's need for social support in living sanely in a world marked by technologically driven changes in life conditions, the inadequacy of facilities for continuing reorientation and renewal, and dwindling community.

But Mannheim was also moved to advocacy of social planning by his awareness of the growing concentration of power in a few key positions to make decisions for whole nations. Mannheim, like many other social theorists of the 20th century, accepted Max Weber's prediction of the inevitable spread of the "iron cage" of bureaucracy in the organization of economic and political affairs.[9] The coordination of large-scale enterprises, Weber argued, requires hierarchical organization and direction of collective effort from a limited number of centers of control. As differentiating technologies have led to further and further specialization of roles, coordination and control of these specialized efforts must be exercised from a few centers, the occupants of which are presumably aware of the larger picture.

Mannheim made an important distinction between two forms of human rationality—functional and substantive.[10] *Functional rationality* refers to the preplanned layout and coordination of

---

[8] See Benne, *The Task of Post-Contemporary Education* (New York: Teachers College Press, 1990), Essay 9, for a discussion of the social roots of widespread contemporary despair and of re-educational ways of moving beyond it.

[9] Max Weber, *The Theory of Social and Economic Organization*.

[10] See Mannheim, *Age of Reconstruction*.

specialized efforts by people working in various roles and departments within an organization. The purpose of such rationalization is to serve more efficiently the goals of the entire organization. In America, Taylorism and "scientific" management are examples of functional rationalization.[11] People whose work has been rationalized do not need to know, much less to control, the bureaucratic ends they are serving or to understand how their efforts contribute to those ends. The system is rationalized in ways that square with the interests of wielders of executive power with the help and advice of expert staff members. Most people in bureaucratized organizations are seen and dealt with as roles interlinked efficiently with other roles rather than as persons dialogically patterning their collective lives. This is the case in bureaucratized organizations, whether they be factories, government agencies, hospitals, or schools.

Functionally rationalized systems do not typically enlist and develop the substantive rationality of most persons working in the system. Substantive rationality refers to the powers of intelligent foresight, thought, choice, and action exercised by persons. *Substantive rationality* is exercised by autonomous persons but is ordinarily developed in dialogic and participative experiences with other persons in communal relationships. This is in line with George Mead's analysis of the origin and growth of selfhood and self-direction.[12] Mannheim advocated the use and development of the substantive rationality of people through their participation in social planning, but did not rid himself of Weber's conviction that the bureaucratization of modern life is inevitable.

Another tendency Mannheim saw in the Age of Invention as it progressed was a drift toward *fundamental democratization*. We accept the truth of his description of the trend but not his naming of it as necessarily "democratization." Mannheim held that "masses" of people in technologically developed societies, increasingly insecure about their future and uncertain about the meaning of their lives, are becoming a major force in political life. Personal insecurity and loss of meaning stem from the eclipse of local, self-sufficient community life and the undermin-

---

[11] See Marvin Weissbord, *Productive Workplaces* (San Francisco: Jossey-Bass, 1987) for a lucid and brief account of Taylorism in American industry and of subsequent moves from it toward democratic workplaces.

[12] George Mead, *Mind, Self and Society* (Chicago: University of Chicago Press, 1931).

ing of traditional ways of social integration and personal socialization. Control of masses of inadequately socialized people requires those in positions of power to woo their support, often by chimeric appeals and threats. The irrational manipulation of mass support has become a major feature of elections in America. Mannheim was well aware of the uses of mass media by those in charge of private and public bureaucracies to manipulate mass opinion and behavior.[13] For him mass media meant radio, because television, communication satellites, and computers had not in his day emerged as social techniques. Monological use of all these tools of imaging and communication has become a much stronger influence on public opinion now than in Mannheim's day. Their possible use in facilitating rational dialogic communication was not often explored then or now. We propose to take that possibility seriously in arguing for reconstructionist views and practices in social life and education. Mannheim, himself a refugee from Nazism, knew that the adroit monologic use of radio was a major factor in the mass phenomena of fascism and Stalinism.

Mannheim did not deal with another important way in which insecure people are now searching for a substitute for uprooted and depotentiated local community living. This is to seek and accept membership in one or another religious sect or ethnic group that requires members to embrace its socially inherited beliefs and practices without question or criticism. Beliefs and rituals are culled from an idealized and idolized past. Fundamentalist groups are active in all modern or modernizing nation-states.

Xenophobia reigns in and among such groups. The drama of life becomes a melodrama. The laws of nation-states with such groups in their populations tend to lose legitimacy when they contravene the certainties on which the perpetuity of these groups depends. Right-to-lifers and born-again biblical literalists in the United States; Sikhs and militant orthodox Hindus in India; Basques in Spain; terrorist Palestinians and West-bank-

---

[13] Mannheim's concept of fundamental "democratization" was much too limited. An important factor in widening and deepening democracy today is the growing incompetence of elite leadership to make effective decisions for society. The growing incompetence of members of the elites arises in part from their biased perspectives. These literally filter out information about the state of society that seriously counters their image of the way society should be. Participatory democracy is an ever more necessary way of governing in order to inform policy decisions that will effectively achieve successful social integration.

settling Zionists in Israel; and the various splintered nations in the former Soviet Union suggest the diversity and the universality of such conflict-and-violence breeding quests for certainty in the 1990s.

Mannheim believed that modernized nations have moved into a new age beyond the age of invention. He did not give a name to this new age of socioeconomic development in which market operations and the maneuvers of nominally democratic (but actually oligarchic) national welfare states are inadequate means to maintain a civilized social life on earth. The age might well be called the Age of Systematic Technological Research and Development (the Age of R & D). Changes in technology and in the conditions of human living no longer depend on chance discovery or dispersed and uncoordinated uses of inventions. All modernized societies have established systems of research and development designed to render obsolete current ways of producing, distributing, and consuming goods and services. Continuing, segmentally planned revolutions in the conditions of living and making a living also require changes in normative cultures, as the prevalence of mass social disease attests. The ruling oligarchies, private and public, that are now waging these technical revolutions, resist the institutionalization of adequate ways for reconstructing normative policies (e.g., democratic planning) that threaten their unilateral power to manage and control. Jurgen Habermas described succinctly the emergence of the age in which we are now living:

> The institutional pressure to augment the productivity of labor through the introduction of new technology has always existed under capitalism, but innovations depended on sporadic inventions. . . . This changed as technical development entered into a feedback relationship with the progress of modern sciences. With the advent of large-scale industrial research, science, technology and industrial utilization were fused into a system. Since then, industrial research has been linked up with research under government, which primarily supports scientific and technical progress in the military sector. From there, information flows back into. . .civilian production. Thus, technology and science become a leading productive force.[14]

---

[14] See Habermas, *Toward a Rational Society*, p. 104.

Habermas suggested an important distinction between system and life world in modern social living. This ties in with the distinction between functional and substantive rationality already discussed. In fact, Habermas subtitled the second volume of his magnum opus *Life World and System: A Critique of Functionalist Reason*.[15] Habermas described the functional rationalization of modern societies as the uncoupling of the economic and political systems from the life worlds of workers and citizens. This requires also the rationalization of life worlds. This can occur only through communicative transactions between autonomous persons, not by their further functional rationalization into systems of roles and relationships. As opposed to Talcott Parsons[16] and other prominent social theorists who attempted to understand and explain society by the one paradigm of *system*, Habermas insisted that two paradigms are needed in order to understand modern societies in their sickness and in their health—system and life world. We agree with Habermas.

Life worlds are coordinated by norms that are maintained by communicative transactions between members of the life world. As uncriticized traditional norms lose their relevance and regulatory authority, and as new norms are required, these can be created, validated, and legitimized only through uncoerced dialogue among members of the life world. Communicative action requires the development and use of the substantive rationality of those who take part in it. A generation before Habermas, Raup and his colleagues, all of them social reconstructionists, defined the goal of normative dialogue (practical judgment) as uncoerced community of persuasion.[17] We agree with McKenney that an adequate communicative ethic is based on consent, not on dead-level consensus.[18] Personal and subcultural differences in style and world view do not disappear in a well-ordered democratic community, but are encouraged and supported.

We have already noted that in a functionally rationalized system, human beings can be induced to perform specialized

---

[15] Jurgen Habermas, *Theory of Communicative Action: A Critique of Functionalist Reason* (Boston: Beacon, 1989).

[16] Talcott Parsons, *The Social System* (New York: The Free Press, 1951).

[17] R. Bruce Raup, George Axtell, Kenneth D. Benne, and B. Othanel Smith, *The Discipline of Practical Judgment in a Democratic Society* (Chicago: University of Chicago Press, 1943).

[18] Gerald McKenny, "From Consensus to Consent: A Plea for a More Communicative Ethic," *Soundings*, 74, (1991), pp. 427–458.

roles with little or no understanding of the goals of the organization in which they are functioning. These goals, as well as the layout of efforts to achieve them, can be set by officials and experts without participation in this setting by most of those induced to conform to the system. This claim is borne out by the substitution of computerized robots for human workers in an increasing number of enterprises. These enterprises include more than factory production and warehouse storage and retrieval—psychotherapy and individualized instruction among them. Psychiatrists and educators too can be technocrats, along with much better paid CEOs.

In oversimple terms, the inducement to conform to system requirements in economic enterprises is money and in political systems it is legal power. A scientific and technocratic mentality has developed and spread among the elites, rulers, and experts, in nations dedicated to military preparedness and dependent on high technology and expensive technological research for achieving the lead against enemy nations. Habermas described this mentality and its relation to the threat of further imbalance between life-world and system aspects of advanced capitalist societies.

> *As such*, the private form of capital utilization and a distribution mechanism for social rewards that guarantees the loyalty of the masses are removed from [public] discussion. . . .Thus arises a perspective in which the development of the social system seems to be determined by the logic of scientific-technical progress. . . .When this semblance has taken root effectively, propaganda can refer to the role of science and technology in order to explain and legitimate why in modern societies the process of democratic decision making about practical problems loses its function and "must" be replaced by plebiscitary decisions about alternative sets of leaders of administrative personnel.[19]

As this technocratic mentality comes to prevail in the thinking and actions of ruling elites in economic and political systems, these elites exert pressure, in Habermasian terms, to "colonize the life worlds" of more aspects of social life. Before discussing further the colonization process and the protest movements that have risen to resist and to reverse it, the distinc-

---

[19] Habermas, *Toward a Rational Society*, p. 105.

tion may be summarized between administrative coordination and control of human conduct in an oligarchic social communicative (political and moral) coordination and control of action in a modern life world. In a society where uncriticized traditions have ceased to furnish an adequate basis for social integration, a life world can be sustained only by ongoing dialogue addressed to the making and remaking of norms to guide collective actions through conflictive situations. The reconstructive dialogue must ideally be joined by all persons affected by the confronting decisions.

By contrast, in a pyramidal organized social system, definition of conflictive situations and their resolution can be worked out by compromises and coalitions between representatives of ruling elites with technical advice from specialized experts. The resolution can then be sold monologically to a majority of the population, often by use of mass media.

Colonization of the life world occurs whenever a sector of social life that has been integrated by agreement among its members, reached through dialogic communication using ordinary language, is functionally rationalized. It may take place through the agency of either a private corporation or a governmental body. In economic systems, linguistic coordination is replaced by the power of money, in governmental colonization, by legal power.

A simple example of the former kind of colonization is the acquisition of a consumers' cooperative store by a grocery chain. Policies for the store had been made and changed in continuing conversations among the store manager, the clerks and the customers at co-op meetings. The connection between management and consumers is now reduced to a cash nexus. Store policies are controlled by impersonal market operations and by a distant central headquarters.

Another example is more fanciful. A corporation offers a cash bonus to employees who spend off-hours at the workplace exercising in the company gymnasium. The exercise is laid out and scheduled by a recreational specialist. The free time of employees is brought under the control of a system. The motivation for such a move might be, in addition to an effort to boost morale, a financial advantage in reduced premiums for health insurance when those covered are guaranteed to be well-exercised employees. This new perquisite might be advertised internally and externally as evidence of the company's personal interest in its employees. We are not against physical exercise or company gymnasia, but are illustrating how double speak may befoul the use of life-world language in promoting the extension of a functionally rationalized system.

An example of life-world colonization by government might be instituting compulsory attendance for preschool children in a Headstart program for a neighborhood in which provision for socialization of young children had been left to families and informal extended family or neighborhood arrangements.

The taking over of a significant part of the socialization of older children and adolescents by compulsory schooling is a good example of life-world colonization, when the school system has been functionally rationalized and bureaucratized. In such schools, students and teachers are fulfilling roles and doing tasks that have been functionally rationalized by administrators and expert staff and sold to parents, teachers, and students monologically. Social reconstructionist educators have always advocated participative planning of school programs in which teachers, parents, and students play a decisive part. This means the decolonization of a system and a return to the condition of a rationalized life world. Recent moves to decentralize school planning in large urban school systems may be a tardy partial acceptance of the wisdom of such advice.

Recently, new social movements have gathered momentum in all functionally rationalized societies. Each of these movements is led by one or more voluntary associations. They are all trying to reorient public opinion by re-educational protests and programs against injustices and other threats engendered by our functionally rationalized and profit-driven political economy. These movements are more complex in their motivations than political parties that seek a greater share in the exercise of governmental power. They are not typical interest groups that seek a greater share of the nation's gross national product by maintaining or changing existing governmental policies, nor do they typically speak in the name of the whole society as totalizing revolutionary or reactionary groups tend to do. They do seek to free oppressed groups from discrimination or domination, to defend and empower some endangered form of life, or to reclaim a life world now colonized by private or public systematization.

The civil rights movement in America, led by African Americans with the help of many persons from other races, is a good example of such new movements in advanced capitalist societies. The movement united in protest persons and groups from diverse socioeconomic classes, various ethnic groups, different religious denominations, and two or more generations. It won concessions from those in power in the American technostructure. At the same time, it served to unify neoconservatives who were frightened and angered rather than re-educated by the protests. Neoconservatives in power are now reneging on these concessions.

The women's movement, the radical ecological movement to maintain the viability of the earth, the movement to limit population growth, the peace movement, and the movement to end discrimination against gays and lesbians are other current examples. Social reconstructionist educators should look kindly on such movements and the voluntary organizations that lead them. The dynamic for re-education and for change from bureaucratic to democratic rule will come from a coalition of such movements, if at all. And educators must try to prevent each of these movements from becoming a single-issue movement. This means an opening of organizations that spearhead various social movements to coalitions in promoting fundamental social changes that will benefit all or several liberation movements.

The radical ecological movement seems most promising in spearheading a coalition around the globe. Survival of the human species can come to be accepted as a good for all people if they hear and accept the message that their own collective and personal conduct is now contributing to species suicide. Benne argued that educators should apply the criterion of "this action of mine or ours contributes to human survival or threatens it" in all their own moral decision making and their own political policymaking and to re-educate others to do the same.[20] This advice assumes that extant life worlds will continue to resist colonization and that some functionally rationalized sectors of society can be reclaimed as democratic life worlds.

Persons are linked to every society, in some large part, by fulfilling shared expectations that are institutionalized as social roles. In a society in which individual effort is treated as a commodity, along with other nonhuman commodities, major roles of persons are defined by others, with little or no input from the role occupant. We have already noted some of the social pathologies that have their origin in this human condition but we have not yet discussed its effect on persons.

---

[20] Benne, "Toward a Moral Basis for Politics and a Political Basis for Morality."

One such effect for many is alienation. In a society in which holding a job is both an economic necessity for most persons and a badge of social acceptability, unemployment connotes alienation. Technological disemployment is an important source of alienation in modernized societies. Skills that workers have spent years in developing are made obsolete when a new technology demands different skills.

The alienation is most painful when robots replace skilled workers in the work of an organization, public or private. This robs the disemployed person of memories of a human career. Their remembered sojourn in society becomes more akin to the manipulation by others of a thing rather than a story of the actions of a person.

A deeply immoral kind of alienation stems from the fetters placed on persons by other-defined roles. The person is alienated from the full development of personal potential that self-direction might have actualized. We have already mentioned the alienation of persons from their substantive rationality by functional rationalization of the workplace and of other agencies on which a person's living depends. Persons are also alienated from potentialities other than their rationality.

Another kind of alienation stems from the elevation of competitiveness as exemplifying human relationship. Ability to compete is seen as a sign of strength. Personal energies tend to be invested in defensive and offensive operations not only against one's enemies but against one's colleagues in winning promotions in rank and pay. Energy spent on defense is unavailable for creative expression and production, whether the defender is a person, an organization, or a nation. There is a paradox here, of course. Teamwork is also lauded in sports, war, and work. But, in each of these, teamwork is instrumental to the real goal of winning by "our side."

Children and young people are separated from older people in productive work. Reproduction of the symbolic culture traditionally depended on cross-age cooperative activities. Exploitation of the labor of children must, of course, be prevented. But the currently long moratorium on youthful productivity tends to both alienate youth from voluntary assumption of responsibility and widen the communication gap between generational groups.

Alienation of these and other sorts abound in advanced capitalist societies. All of them tend to distort both the development of autonomous persons and effective processes of cultural reproduction and renewal. Mannheim came to believe that human beings can no longer depend on spontaneous adjustments that once enabled them, during the Age of Invention, to muddle through social dislocations precipitated by adoption of new technologies with concomitant changes in life conditions. In our Age of R & D, conscious, deliberate, and intentional "revolutions" in life conditions are being engendered by haphazard utilization of new science-based technologies. Institutional ways of controlling and coordinating the uses or nonuses of such technologies must also become conscious, deliberate, and intentional. To such processes of control and coordination, Mannheim (1943) gave the name of planning.

> We are living in an age of transition from *laissez faire* to a planned society. The planned society that will come may take one of two shapes. It will be ruled by a minority in terms of a dictatorship or a new form of government which, in spite of its increased power, will still be democratically controlled.[21]

We too believe that there must be a transformation of political economies that are now steered by allegedly competitive market operations with inept regulation of multinational corporate ventures by the governments of nation-states. There must be an institutionalization of democratic planning in inventing the future, if there is indeed to be a future for humankind on earth. This does not mean that market operations in setting prices and allocating capital investments will disappear completely from a planning society. Some aspects of economic production and distribution may well be best left to market operations. But which aspects of economic life will be left under control by market operations will be determined by democratic planning.

A CRITIQUE OF MANNHEIM

We find two major interrelated faults in Mannheim's conception of a democratically planned society. The first of these is his

---

[21] Karl Mannheim, *Diagnosis of Our Time* (New York: Humanities Press, 1941), p. 1.

apparent identification of democracy with meritocracy and representative government. The second is his acceptance of Max Weber's conviction that bureaucracy is the inevitable form of human organization in an industrialized society, along with Michel's consonant "iron law of oligarchy."[22] In keeping with this assumption, Mannheim argued that planning decisions must be made from a limited number of positions in a society, not by dialogically engendered, communal consent of all affected by the plan.

Mannheim argued that the work of preparing plans and ways of administering plans belongs to expert scientists, technical experts, economists, and other social scientists. These groups will consult with leaders of various interest groups and with governmental leaders in developing proposed plans. But, in effect, an elite group of planners would define the historical situation and set the agenda for public discussion of proposed priorities in dealing with the challenges of that situation as they define it. Mannheim considered such control of public discussion by elites and their behind-the-scene preparation of proposed plans to be necessary for coherent parliamentary debate and decision.

Modern representative governments, as we have already argued, are actually oligarchies, though their publicists may call them democracies. In a democracy, those affected by a policy must participate in all phases of policymaking—initiation, maturation, and decision. Mannheim's vesting of an elite with power to initiate plans is meritocratic rather than democratic. But he was conscious of a danger to popular control in his proposed way of planning. He knew that his proposal gave massive power to the planners and that the exercise of that power should be enlightened and socially responsible. This concern he expressed as a question: "Who is to plan the planners?" His tentative answer to this question is quite inadequate. Mannheim proposed that the "class" (but to him not really a social class) of intellectuals would be useful in making planners aware of and responsible for the consequences of their proposed plans, if and when these are put into practice.

Intellectuals, Mannheim believed, because they are not in contention with other strata and interest groups for augmented power in society, can analyze and evaluate proposed plans in a relatively disinterested way. They can develop both ideological

---

[22] Roberto Michels, *Political Parties* (New York: The Free Press, 1944).

(conservative) and utopian (radical) critiques of proposed plans. Particular intellectuals may be biased by the limiting perspective of the class that grants them patronage. But because intellectuals as a whole reflect all the various perspectives in a society, they may provide comparatively "above-the-battle," dependable information about the meanings of plans in action for use by the planners and by the parliaments that will legitimize preferred plans.

Our criticism of this somewhat fanciful idea is based on the sociology of knowledge, a branch of social theory in which Mannheim was a doughty pioneer.[23] The absence of a psychological appetite for greater power from intellectuals does not deprive them of particular perspectives or endow them with a generalized perspective. Perspectives emerge from communicative participation in one life world or another. Intellectuals, like other mortals, socially inherit points of view in some such way, and the points of view of their patrons also affect their views on issues.

In contemporary societies, the principal patrons of intellectuals are universities. In the present climate of bureaucratized universities, scholarly work tends to be specialized to the point of compartmentalization, both in its content and in the vocabularies in which its results are published. Only a few intellectuals focus their substantive rationalities on questions of public policy. We fear that university-based intellectuals have lost whatever free-floating and synthesizing capabilities intellectuals may have once possessed. Intellectuals employed by partisan "think tanks" are, for the most part, propagandists, who are quite incapable of helping to define or serve a common interest in matters under dispute.

Our answer to Mannheim's question—"Who is to plan the planners?"—is different from his. All stakeholders in any given plan will participate in planning, dialogically define the common interest in their human situation, and utilize and direct the services of relevant experts in making and implementing plans to advance that interest. We are quite aware that stakeholders in plans to maintain the viability of the earth for human and other diverse forms of life are coincident with the population of the world. All people in our polyglot, stratified, divided, segregated, and hostile world should ideally participate in planning for the survival of the human species. We argue later that such participa-

---

[23] Karl Mannheim, *Ideology and Utopia* (New York: Harcourt Brace, 1937).

tion, however difficult, is now possible, though it may not have been when Mannheim wrote a half-century ago.

We have already noted that Mannheim, like Weber and Michels, believed bureaucratic organization to be inevitable in modern societies. We disagree. Our case against bureaucracy has, for the most part, been made in earlier discussion of the social and personal ills that stem from rampant functional rationalization of public and private administrations. Benne (1990) stated the case against bureaucratic organization.[24] Such organizations are unable:

> To respond flexibly and mindedly to external and internal demands for changes in goals and methods of achieving them. Yet change is the predominant quality of life in contemporary societies and an expectation for the future. The inabilities of bureaucrats]. . .to assess needs for change and to plan and effect changes in roles, rules, internal and external relations, and methods of operation are due to several features of bureaucratic organization. It is not alone their large size. Their pyramidal structure, with decisions concentrated at the top of the pyramid; their mechanical assignment of partial tasks to segregated departments, which operate without awareness of or responsibility for the. . .mission of the organization; their dependence for the motivation of persons on external rewards rather than on commitment to the purposes of the organization—all of these make for inflexible, mindless and dehumanized operations.[25]

Harrington argued that it was bureaucratic organization that perverted the professed democratic ideals of Marxian socialism in Stalinist Soviet Union.[26] Actually, totalitarian societies are bureaucracies writ large, trying to define and control, not just the work roles of members from a central headquarters. Horizontal communication is fettered in the interest of unhampered central control. Technical information is hoarded by those in the top

---

[24] Kenneth D. Benne, *The Task of Post-Contemporary Education* (New York: Teachers College Press, 1990).

[25] See Kenneth D. Benne, "Man and Moloch," In *Education for Tragedy* (Lexington: University of Kentucky Press, 1967), p. 18, for an account of the dehumanizing effects on role occupants of life in a totalizing bureaucracy.

[26] Michael Harrington, *Socialism* (New York: Bantam Books, 1972).

echelons. Information about the failures and successes of plans as tried and about the morale of citizens tend to be skewed toward what those at the top wish to hear. Plans are bound to be faulty. Communication with persons and groups who interpret events from differing viewpoints is intentionally limited in order to protect the official ideology from doubt and subversion. In this way, learning and change are inhibited. Similar processes of domination occur in all bureaucracies, whether they define and control one or several social roles of members. All persons in our democratic oligarchy are living some part of their lives in the "iron cage," as Max Weber termed it, of one bureaucracy or another.

Students of organizational behavior have recently confirmed the advantages democratization can bring to the workplace. When decision making is pushed downward from the center, when workers participate responsibly in decisions about their work, productivity and quality of product improve. Participative management is now practiced in a number of "enlightened" corporations. Slater and Bennis (1964), both first-rate students of organizational life, became enamored enough of this trend in corporate management to declare in print that "Democracy Is Inevitable."[27] Any claim of inevitability in history is, of course, a denial of history, as every post-Hegelian philosopher knows. But, more empirically, these authors forgot that workplace democracy in our economy is a delegation from those in power; a privilege, not a right. Nor did they seem to notice that some multinationals that are most "enlightened" in their internal management practices are potent agents of domination in their relation to workers in the Third World. They might, more truly and hopefully, have titled their piece "Bureaucracy Is Not Inevitable."

Morgan recognized six types of rulership in organizational life—autocracy, bureaucracy, technocracy, codetermination by several elites, representative democracy, and direct democracy.[28] We have postulated that rulership in America and in other developed nations is a coalescence between bureaucracy, technocracy, and codetermination. Representative democracy has become oligarchy. This coalescence should be superseded by movement toward direct democracy. We would, of course, seek to

---

[27] Philip Slater and Warren Bennis, "Democracy is Inevitable," *Harvard Business Review*, 42, (1964) pp. 51–59.

[28] Gareth Morgan, *Images of Organization* (Beverly Hills, CA: Sage, 1985).

maintain representative democracy's bill of rights, along with its febrile attempts to feel the mass pulse by expensive polling and survey research, during the long and chancy period of re-education and social experimentation that will be necessary to bring globewide direct democracy into full operation.

TECHNOLOGY AND A PLANNING DEMOCRACY

We have argued for the desirability of democratic participation in making effective plans and policies. But is such a democracy possible in dealing with problems that have become global in scope? The commonly held idea that it is impossible stems in part from unimaginative views of the possible uses of technologies now available or in the process of development. When Robert Michels proclaimed his "iron law of oligarchy," he did not contend that it is rooted in some inherent superiority of the oligarchs over those they rule.[29] Rather, he grounded the law in requirements for efficient organization of human enterprises. His argument was not unlike that of James Madison in the *Federalist Papers* against direct democracy for the national government. Such democracy was impossible because of limitations in transportation and communication. In Madison's time, technologies for ultrasonic velocities in transportation and virtually instantaneous communication of information around the earth were not extant. Aristotle had once argued for limitation of the size of the Greek polis to an area that a herald might traverse during one day in announcing an assembly of citizens.

Over the years, the most convincing arguments for the necessity of representative or oligarchic rule and against the practicability of direct democracy have been based on assumptions about the availability and the use of pertinent technologies. The economizing advantages of hierarchy in the storage and transmission of information do not result only from large distances to be spanned or in large populations to be involved. They pertain also to the density of events within limited spaces. Imagine a busy factory crowded with people in bustling activities. It would not do to have everybody rushing about, bumping into each other, in

---

[29] Roberto Michels, *Political Parties* (New York: The Free Press, 1944).

order to consult with each other in coordinating their work. It seems clearly more economical to assign a few people to the tasks of coordination and transmission of information and to reduce the number of routes over which information is passed by having those few people report to and transmit orders from a central office. It would seem impossible to locate bulky files of information at every workstation and far more economical to store them in a central headquarters. It follows that occupants of the central office have more ready access to relevant information than do others in the workplace, and readier access to relevant information means greater power to make informed decisions for all.

The capital costs of storing, retrieving, transmitting, and receiving information, through visual images and spoken words, are still high, but are being reduced with breathtaking rapidity. And, perhaps of greater importance, the technologies of our information era are becoming more accessible for use by local groups, organizations, and neighborhoods. More workplaces, households, conference facilities, and local meeting places will soon be able to acquire efficient devices for transmitting and receiving images, ideas, and information to and from others, near and far. Primitive beginnings have already been made in using new technologies dialogically rather than monlogically, or the exchange of opinions and viewpoints among peers. Radio and television call-in shows now typically serve as media for catharsis by the alienated. But they have in their pattern the germ of responsible communication between peers with diverse views on conflictive issues of common concern.

The costs of storing, retrieving, and processing information are also plummeting downward. Small, inexpensive, user-friendly computers are now available and linkage of computers into networks has spread. Large master computers can now be accessed and, in some cases, programmed by small computers anywhere on Earth and from all around it. These developments open possibilities for direct popular participation in social-economic deliberations and decision making. Access to dependable relevant information is of great importance, but information must be interpreted in defining action situations and in assessing action alternatives. Interpretation involves the surfacing of normative orientations as well as scientific knowledge and technical know-how. Persons and groups become conscious of their own distinctive perspectives only when challenged by conflicting viewpoints out of which others interpret their worlds. Self-reflective dialogue is necessary for understanding and appreciation of differences in perspectives, for thoughtful consideration of alternatives, and for attaining consent, not dead-level consensus, to some optimal resolution of confronting issues. Such creative bargaining is, of necessity, a group and intergroup affair.

Electronic technology can now be used to facilitate the formation of groups. Computerized dating services have shown the way. People can enter their need for partners into a computer and be matched with others of like interests and proclivities. There is no reason why a similar process can not be used to assemble local or global groups with members of like mind. Such groups can inform and enrich their deliberations on issues with needed expertise or with similar or different views on issues under consideration.

The combination of open access to computer-stored information, computer matching services, instantaneous translation, and instantaneous dialogic communication between persons and groups offer the possibility of organizing from below, of initiating agenda for debate and discussion and of participating in the dialogic resolution of issues on the public agenda. People no longer need hegemonic definition of action situations and resolution of conflictive issues by officials in a higher position in one hierarchy or another. The same technologies make possible the formation of communication between scientific, aesthetic, spiritual, hobby, and politico-economic groups across cultural and subcultural boundaries as well.[30]

---

[30] We should not overlook the dark side of the technological interdependence that has been achieved in our Age of R & D. It has brought with it threats to the survival of modern civilization, perhaps of all terrestrial life. The earth's ever more interdependent economic and financial systems are increasingly dependent on computer networks. These can be accessed and reprogrammed by increasing numbers of unauthorized persons. Computer hacking and infection by computer viruses can become a new form of guerrilla warfare. Relatively small groups of disaffected and alienated people are acquiring the technical capability of bringing the world's processes of production and distribution to an abrupt halt. Given the systematic connections between the military establishments of various nations and the defense industries, and between these industries and peacetime industries, it is quite believable that computer sabotage from below might work its way into unauthorized command of nuclear missiles. The notion that there exists a permanent "fix" for the security problem seems to ignore the fact that the solution will be an electronic solution as the problem itself is, technically speaking, and that there is no way of limiting the spread of the knowledge and skills involved. The best answer, as we have noted before, is not technical but re-educational. The ruling elites must learn to share power, and the alienated must learn to communicate with each other and with their former oppressors.

Crises of motivation and legitimation, and the pathologies of alienation that are endemic in advanced capitalist societies must be worked through dialogically if civilized life is to survive on earth, indeed if the earth is to remain viable for any form of life. Participative planning by all people in shaping their future is now necessary as an alternative to bureaucratic organization of human life and work and to oligarchic rule of masses of people by coalitions of elites. We cannot, of course, foretell what institutional infrastructure planning by people in a global democracy will require or how the old infrastructures will be superseded. But we do claim that such changes have become feasible through imaginative and democratic uses of available and developable technologies. Direct democracy can no longer rationally be dismissed as a figment of social reconstructionists' imagination, their impossible dream.

The vision of a democratically planning society, active at local, regional. national, and global levels, should be seen as a universally acceptable moral ideal and criterion. Those who would effectively criticize and change outmoded institutions and ideologies need ideals. We recommend the ideal of global democratic planning in the spirit of two early social reconstructionists, Benne and Stanley (1939), who argued for "empirically transcendent ideals" in their recommendations to educators living and working within a crisis culture. They were responding to two quite different, then and now extant, views of ideals. Some scientistic philosophers denied meaning to ideals for which we have no currently available tested operations to bring them into actuality. Other philosophers believed that transcendent ideals must be grounded in extra-human reality beyond history. Benne and Stanley argued for the crucial importance of "empirically transcendent" ideals:

> We have asserted the importance [but the inadequacy] of scientific evaluation of alternative techniques and programs to re-equilibrate a society harboring a change in basic purposes. The only possible alternative to [violent] struggle in such a case seems to us to lie in the enunciation within that culture of an adequate and inclusive moral ideal. . . .The problem is no less a problem than that of reorienting and reconceiving the most fundamental interests and postulates of society in a way to unite . . . clashing interests and ideals into a wider and more inclusive [dia-

logue].... Such is the task of moral vision, of the ... moral prophet.[31]

It is in this spirit that we offer the ideal of a global democratic planning society to Earth's citizens and more especially to educators.

RE-EDUCATION FOR THE 21ST CENTURY

Albert Einstein suggested as succinctly as anyone the vast re-educative task that recent developments in mastery of our physical environment have placed on our generation: "The unleashed power of the atom has changed every thing save our modes of thinking, and we thus drift toward unparalleled catastrophes."[32] Einstein recommended his implied agenda to educators when nuclear holocaust seemed the most probable way in which mankind might effect its own suicide. Additional ways of rendering all life extinct of which we have become aware underline the wisdom of his implied advice to earth's people: "Re-educate your basic modes of thinking or perish."

The truth of John Dewey's (1937) terse comment concerning education and schooling should be recognized by all educators in the 21st century: "School education is but one educative agency out of many, and at the best is a minor educational force."[33] The development of persons from infancy to death is patterned by many institutions in addition to schooling—families, day-care centers, neighborhoods, play places, workplaces, mass media, entertainment, friendships, professional associations, political campaigns, wars and other violence, and gossipy recitations of old wives' tales. (Some tale-tellers are old husbands, too.) Education, when taken as another name for enculturation, incorporates all these influences that perpetuate society and

---

[31] Kenneth D. Benne and William O. Stanley, II, "The Nature and Social Function of Moral Ideals," *Social Frontier*, 5, (1939), pp. 167–170.

[32] Albert Einstein, *Einstein on Peace* (New York: Simon & Schuster, 1960), p. 376.

[33] John Dewey, "Education and Social Change," *Social Frontier*, 3, (1937), p. 235.

socialize persons. *Education*, in this usage, includes miseducation as well as praiseworthy education.

Educators, responsive to the social reconstructionist ideal, should become informed critics of the processes of enculturation in their own country and beyond. Their critical advice should become available for all enculturating agencies, not just to schools. This will require a redeployment of the services of educators far beyond agencies that are now typically labeled educational. Educators should work to build bridges of mutual understanding among various agencies of socialization. Cooperation among socializing agencies will not bring dead-level uniformity to educational policies and programs but will rather bring conflicts between the goals and assumptions of various agencies of education into the open. Today, they are hidden from public view by specialization, bureaucratic organization, and propaganda from the ruling elites. The task of educators is to bring conflicting parties into the dialogue, into creative bargaining concerning their differences, and into the creation of new practices to which those now in conflict can consent.

Benne pointed out over 50 years ago that every society incorporates two groups of persons who need help in becoming productive members of society and in functioning as autonomous persons within it.[34] One group is the chronologically immature. The other is made up of those who are alienated from full participation in societal life. Educators always have two missions—shaping the development of the young and reduction of alienation of persons of all ages. In the Age of Discovery, the drama of conscious socialization could well focus on bringing ever-new crops of barbarians in our midst—children and young people—into viable societal membership. In such societies, education could, with only minimal distortion, be identified with pedagogy. Adequate models for future human development lay within the past.

The task of education has changed radically through the 20th century. The need for continued education and re-education of persons throughout their life spans has risen to an unprecedented crescendo. All of us have become aliens in our relentlessly changing world, our Age of R & D. Benne urged that educators think of their professional practice not as pedagogy but as anthropology—help in the re-education of persons of all ages.[35]

---

[34] See Benne, *A Conception of Authority*.
[35] See Benne, *The Task of Post-Contemporary Education*.

We must invent adequate models for life in an unprecedented future, while we maintain continuity with that which is still valuable in our traditional wisdom, with special emphasis on our democratic traditions.

Educators can locate places in their culture where change is most needed by identifying the cultural conflicts that most deeply divide people. Re-educators will do well to remember that conflict unites as well as divides persons and groups from diverse and discrepant cultures and subcultures. They should focus their re-educational efforts on conflicts between people, not on what is agreed upon by persons on all sides of current conflicts. The purpose of re-educational effort is to engender dialogue between persons and groups now in conflict. The dialogue, to be fully re-educative, must be uncoerced. It must point toward mutual understanding of those now in conflict. It must be informed with the best available and relevant knowledge of act–consequence relationships and simultaneously be focused on the reconciliation of discrepant norms and value orientations.

Such dialogic processes are at one and the same time democratic and re-educative. They are alternative to settling conflicts by violence. In our age of high tech, including nuclear weaponry, no side can win any war. We must learn nonviolent ways of resolving conflicts and prominent in all such ways should be re-educative dialogue. We must learn our way into a future that has only one certainty in it—the certainty that future living will be different from the way in which we now live.

In urging on educators the necessity of lifelong learning, a change of focus from pedagogy to anthropology in their conception of educational practice, we are not discounting the importance of early childhood education. We are rather claiming that early childhood education will not be redeemed until the adults with major influence on its goals and methods are themselves re-educated. Children encounter conflicts as they live, work, and play with other children and with adults. Conflicts between diverse actors always present learning opportunities. Those in conflict, if they can be joined in discussion of their diverse interest and viewpoints, can learn of life worlds different from their own, become more conscious and self-critical of their own prejudices, and learn nonviolent ways of resolving conflicts. Yet, typically, in schools and out, adults settle conflicts between children by police methods, by coercively restoring law and order.

Social reconstructionists hold that contemporary education and re-education should focus on the teaching and learning of contemporary conflicts. Local conflicts frequently are related to regional, national, and global conflicts. For example, children and young people face a conflict between driving their own automobiles and using public transportation in traveling. This may seem a local question, a family question perhaps, and a question of economic costs. But, seen properly, it leads also into the earthwide problem of limiting the burning of fossil fuels and arresting processes of global warming. Becoming responsible world citizens in our Age of R & D requires consciousness of the connection between personal and local habits of consumption, with transnational actions to avert species suicide. Such raising of consciousness becomes likely only when value-laden conflicts become the focus of deliberate education. Persons and groups in conflict achieve community as they join in dialogue addressed to the conflicts that now threaten and divide them. Conducting such dialogue becomes a central task for 21st-century educators, whether they are working in scholastic or nonscholastic situations.

In inventing and practicing nonviolent ways of conflict resolution, educators and educands are united methodologically not by common and uniform substantive life orientations and devotions. The latter are now and will remain diverse and the former should become common. Learning a methodology is not learning a mechanical calculus for turning out tidy answers to neatly formulated problems. Methodological characters incorporate and develop habits of mind, virtues of thoughtfulness, in persons and in the norms of their associations. These come into consciousness as persons define and judge life worlds that conflict with their socially inherited normative orientations. Raup and his colleagues made an important beginning in defining the methodological character needed by persons in making wise practical judgments in a crisis culture.[36] Their suggestions have been only partially carried forward and improved in continuing studies of critical thinking by educators.

Habits of mind that contribute to hegemonic relations and a ready resort to coercive and violent ways of dealing with diversity lie deep within the thinking of all of us. Only rigorous self-reflection and self-criticism will bring them into conscious focus. Communicative participation across cultural boundaries

---

[36] See Raup, *The Discipline of Practical Judgment in a Democratic Society.*

is the prime setting in which self-reflection and self-criticism occur. Two habits of mind that are rampant in America's ethnically diverse society undergird the proneness to destructive violence that also characterizes life in America. Both of these militate against an education oriented to the building of a global community. We are certain that other national cultures are now transmitting habits of mind that are equally inimical to such education, but self-criticism should begin at home.

Persons in America from one subcultural enclave or another learn early to move readily from encounters with others who are different to a judgment of the others' worth. Are they better or worse than we are? We tend to rank people as we confront differences between *them* and *us*. This habit underlies our devotion to grading systems in schools—students in a classroom cannot be all As or all Fs. Competition is the only reliable way of motivating students to work. It also underlies our obsession with competitiveness and with winning in competitions in games and in economic affairs. Those who are markedly different are prejudged to be inferior or alternatively to be adversaries, not as possibly superior in some respects, inferior in others, and as potential collaborators from whom we might learn and who might learn from us. When we aim to increase cooperation in an organization, we set up a competition between groups and give prizes to the group that is most cooperative. At times, we seem not to find inherent value in our own way of life. This preconscious American habit of mind must be surfaced, criticized, and re-educated if community is to function for us as the ideal organization of human work and play.

When our habit of ranking differences is combined with preconscious assumptions about strength as the power to compel the obedience of others, the outcome tends to be ready resort to violent ways of dealing with diversity and conflict. Gaining strength, when it is defined in this way, is akin to arming for battle—handguns for children, AK-47s for young adults, and nuclear missiles for grown-ups in the Department of Defense. This habit of mind is evident in resistance by current majorities to equal rights for various minorities in areas of oppression—men over women, Whites over African Americans, and straights over gays. It is evident also in international relations with technologically underdeveloped countries. The United States will extend a helping hand only to nations that have economies similar to our own or will require—as we so often do—that other nations "restructure" their economies to meet our needs. For, self-evidently, alien ways are inferior to our own and we are stronger (have more powerful weapons) than they have.

We are not denying, of course, that contact with an alien culture may at times be a threat to a cherished way of life. But it is also an opportunity to explore another way of living and a different, perhaps a more fulfilling, outlook on life. Encounter with difference may result in welcome growth on the part of both in the encounter. There are no doubt other "habits of mind" in American culture that require self-reflection and re-education. Re-education does not lead necessarily to new habits of mind, but may lead to reconfirmation of traditional modes of thinking that have fallen out of fashion in our Age of R & D. Social reconstructionist education is not a creation of a new culture and of new persons. Rather, it incorporates creative and critical processes of personal, institutional, and cultural renewal. Because all of Earth's cultures are in need of renewal in this last decade of the 20th century, we recommend social reconstructionist thought and practice to educators in the 21st century.

AUTHOR INDEX

A

Alexander, F., 121, 122
Anderson, J., 111
Anderson, M., 7
Apple, M.W., 4, 5, 7–9, 12, 15–17, 21–26, 31
Aronowitz, S., 44, 55
Astuto, T., 9, 15
Axtell, G., 152
Ayer, E., 118

B

Bastian, A., 8, 25
Benne, K.D., 52, 142, 143, 148, 152, 156, 161, 167, 168
Bennett, K., 10, 13
Bennett, W.J., 3, 4
Bennis, W., 162
Bliven, B., 46
Bode, B.H., 37, 38
Boles, K., 24
Bowers, C.A., 29, 45, 48, 52, 113
Bowles, S., 7, 14, 16
Brameld, T., 32
Bromley, S., 10, 13
Brooks, V.W., 58, 59
Burlbau, L., 116, 119
Burnham, W.D., 11

C

Callahan, R., 30
Camp Edwards, A., 90
Camp Mayhew, K., 90
Carbone, P.F., Jr., 57, 65
Carnoy, M., 55
Chambliss, J.J., 37
Childs, J., 38
Christian-Smith, L., 26
Clark, D., 9, 15
Cloward, R., 9
Cobb Jordan, E., 132
Cookson, P.W., Jr., 92
Corradi, J., 41
Counts, G.S., 46, 47, 53, 66, 89, 114
Cremin, L.A., 30, 48, 87, 89, 94, 104
Curti, M., 32

D

de Lima, A., 43, 47
Dennis, L., 84
Dewey, E., 89
Dewey, J., 29, 36, 37, 44, 89, 167
Dworkin, M.S., 90, 95, 102

E

Eaton, W., 51
Einstein, A., 167

F

Feinberg, W., 29
Fierman, J., 107
Franklin, B., 116
Freedman, S., 24
Fruchter, N., 8, 25

G

Gambrill, J.M., 65
Giarelli, J., 113
Gibson Buis, A., 130
Gintis, H., 5–7, 16
Giroux, H., 4, 44, 55
Gittell, M., 8, 25
Goodenow, R., 115
Goodwyn, L., 40
Graham, P.A., 31
Greer, C., 8, 25
Gutek, G., 48

H

Habermas, J., 146, 151–153
Hall, S., 9–13, 21, 25, 119, 120
Hansot, E., 46, 107, 112, 131
Harding, V., 22
Harrington, M., 161
Harrison, 32, 37
Haskins, K., 8, 25
Hogan, D., 22
Hook, S., 32, 34–36, 49
Howe, I., 28
Hunter, A., 12–14, 19–21

I

Irwin, M.F., 111

J

Jackson, J., 24
Jacques, M., 10
James, M., 116, 121, 125
Jenkinson, E., 44
Jessop, B., 10, 13
Judis, J.B., 44

K

Kilpatrick, W.H., 49, 52, 54, 114
Klehr, H., 49
Kliebard, H., 116
Krueger, L., 68

L

Larrain, J., 9
Laski, 48
Leap, W., 112
Lemann, N., 110
Levin, H., 55
Lewis, E., 110
Ling, T., 10, 13
Link, W., 115, 118
Lloyd, S.M., 89, 104–106
Lowe, R., 46, 112, 131

M

Mannheim, K., 145, 148, 158, 160
McKenny, G., 152
Mead, G., 149
Meier, D.W., 44, 45
Mendenhall, J.E., 67, 77
Michels, R., 159, 163
Morgan, G., 162
Murphy, M., 130, 131, 134
Murray, J.W., 92

O

O'Coin, A.R., 131
Omi, M., 10, 14–19, 22, 23

P

Parsons, T., 152
Parkhurst, H., 97–99
Peeler, D.P., 110
Persell, C.H., 92
Piccone, P., 41
Picott, J.R., 111
Piven, F., 9
Poulantzas, N., 39
Pratt, C., 89, 92–94, 96

R

Raskin, M., 9, 14
Raup, R.B., 152, 170
Record, W., 125
Richardson, A., 129, 133
Rose, S., 3
Rosener, J.B., 107
Rugg, H., 60–87

S

Schafer, J., 66
Scott, H., 61
Seideman, D., 45, 49
Semel, S.F., 97, 99, 101
Sequel, M.L., 116, 119
Shor, I., 55, 56
Shores, J.H., 87
Shumaker, A., 85
Slater, P., 162
Smith, B.O., 87, 152
Smith, G.E., 131

Sprague Mitchell, L., 89
Stanley, W.O., 87, 167
Swain, M., 131

T

Tindall, G., 114, 115
Trotter, J.W., Jr., 110
Tushnet, M., 136
Tyack, D., 46, 107, 112, 131

U

Urban, W., 45, 48

V

Veblen, T., 61

W

Wallace, J.M., 43
Warren, D., 48
Warren, F., 49
Weber, M., 146, 148
Wechsler, 53
Weissbord, M., 149
Westbrook, R., 41, 96
Wilson, E., 32
Wilson, V.S., 65
Winant, H., 10, 14–19, 22, 23
Woelfel, N., 55
Woodson, C., 111

SUBJECT INDEX

A

Affirmative action, 7, 16
African American, 13, 16–18, 20, 23, 109–138, 155–156
"Age of Discovery" (Mannheim), 145, 168
"Age of Invention" (Mannheim), 145–150, 158
"Age of Systematic Technological Research and Development" (The Age of R&D), 151, 158, 165ff, 168, 170, 172
Alienation, 157–158
American Federation of Teachers, 51, 55, 124, 130–134
American League for Peace and Democracy, 52
American Student Union, 52
America's Coming of Age (Van Wyck Brooks), 58
Authoritarian populism, 10

B

The Bookworm's Digest, 94
Bureaucratic organization, 140, 144, 159–162
nonbureaucratic, 140, 162

C

Censorship, textbooks, 30, 44
Child-centered education, 47, 87, 90–108, 113
The Child-Centered School (Harold Rugg), 87
City and Country School, 91–96
The Clearing House, 121–122
Conservatism, *see* New Right
Culture and Education in America (Harold Rugg), 59
Curriculum, socially reconstructive, 116–129

D

The Dalton School, 91, 96–102, 108

E

Ecological crisis, 141–142, 144
pollution, 141–142
Ecological movement, 156–157
The Educational Frontier (William H. Kilpatrick), 48
Equality, 3–5, 7, 19, 21, 25
civil equality, 6

F

Federal aid to education, *see* Harrison-Black-Fletcher bill
Foundations of American Education (Harold Rugg), 87
Functional rationality, 148–149, 152–155
Fundamental democratization, occurring in Mannheim's "Age of Invention," 149–150
Fundamentalist groups, 150–151

G

George Peabody College, 116–117
Great Depression, 7, 29, 45–46, 48, 55, 64, 103, 109–138, 140
The Great Technology (Harold Rugg), 61–81, 84

H

Harrison-Black-Fletcher bill, 129–136
Hull House, 103

I

Indoctrination, 30, 33–42, 45–46, 47–48, 50, 51, 53
Intelligence tests, 60, 123, 126–127
Interdependence, 141

J

Jefferson, Thomas, School for Social Science, 124
John Dewey Society, 29

L

Labor-capital compromise, 14
Letters and Leadership (Van Wyck Brooks), 59
Lincoln School, at Teachers College, 65

M

"Man-as-Artist," *see* Redemption through the Arts
Marxism, 31–33, 79, 113, 122, 161

N

The Nation, 45–46, 49, 50, 52
National Association for the Advancement of Colored People (NAACP), 130–136
National Education Association, 55, 130–137
Negro Organization Society, 132
Neo-conservatism, *see* New Right
New Deal, 29, 64, 74, 80, 131
　Agricultural Adjustment Act, 74
　National Recovery Act, 74
　Tennessee Valley Authority, 80–81
New Masses, 46
The New Republic, 43, 45–48, 49
New Right, 1–26, 142, 156
　core curriculum, 3
　evangelical schooling, 2–3
　morals, 4
　restoration of conservatism, 23–24

P

Participative democracy, 143–144
The People's Voice, 124
Planned communities, 147–148
Planned economy, 60, 158–167
Play, as pedagogy, 92–93
Plessy "separate but equal" ruling, 111
Politics of culture, 144
Progressive education, 29, 31, 54, 87–88, 89–91, 112
Progressive Education Association, 29, 31, 45
Property rights versus person rights, 5–8, 16–17

R

"Redemption Through the Arts," 85–87
Rethinking Schools, 25
"Reverse discrimination, 3

S

The School and Society (John Dewey), 90
Scientific management, *see* functional rationality
Secular humanism, 3, 8, 44
The Seven Arts, 60
Shady Hill School, 103
Share Croppers Union, 114
Social class, 32, 34–37, 44, 46, 48, 49, 68–71, 93, 113, 159
 classless society, 34–35, 55
Social engineering, 58, 82–83
Social Frontier, 27–42, 51, 130
Social studies, 60–81
Southern Coalition for Educational Equity, 25
Substantive rationality, 149, 160
Support groups, 147–148
Standards, 4, 8
 academic, 3, 8
 teacher licensing, 8

T

Teacher salaries, 111–112, 135–136
Teachers College, 28, 60, 119, 124
Technology, 141–143, 151–154, 157–161, 163–176
 technological disemployment, 157
 as a tool for democratic planning, 163–172

V

Virginia, social reconstruction in, 109–138
Virginia Curriculum Revision Project, 118–130
 curricular aims, 119–129
 Tentative Course of Study for the Elementary Schools, 127
Virginia Education Association, 118
Virginia State College for Negroes, 118
Virginia State Teachers Association, 123–124, 134–136
Voucher plans, 8, 21

W

Women's movement, 17, 18, 156
Women, as progressive
  administrators, 89
  paradox as authoritarian
    managers, 95–96, 100–102,
    105–106
  as democratic leaders, 107–108

Y

Young Communist League, 53